THE SPANISH CIVIL WAR

ANDREW FORREST

ROUTLEDGE

London and New York

First published 2000
by Routledge
11 New Fetter Lane, London EC4P 4EE

Simultaneously published in the USA and Canada
by Routledge
29 West 35th Street, New York, NY 10001

Routledge is an imprint of the Taylor & Francis Group

Typeset in Grotesque and Perpetua
by Keystroke, Jacaranda Lodge, Wolverhampton
Printed and bound in Great Britain by Clays Ltd, St Ives plc

British Library Cataloguing in Publication Data
A catalogue record for this book is available from the British Library

Library of Congress Cataloging in Publication Data
Forrest, Andrew, 1947–
    The Spanish Civil War / Andrew Forrest.
      p.   cm. – (Questions and analysis in history)
    Includes bibliographical references (p.) and index.
    1. Spain–History–Civil War, 1936–1939. I. Title. II. Series.
    DP269.F62 2000
    946.081–dc21   99–056393

ISBN 0–415–18211–5

To my parents with love and gratitude for their
friendship and encouragement

CONTENTS

ILLUSTRATIONS

SERIES PREFACE

Most history textbooks now aim to provide the student with interpretation, and many also cover the historiography of a topic. Some include a selection of sources.

So far, however, there have been few attempts to combine all the skills needed by the history student. Interpretation is usually found within an overall narrative framework and it is often difficult to separate the two for essay purposes. Where sources are included, there is rarely any guidance as to how to answer the questions on them.

The Questions and Analysis series is therefore based on the belief that another approach should be added to those which already exist. It has two main aims.

The first is to separate narrative from interpretation so that the latter is no longer diluted by the former. Most chapters start with a background narrative section containing essential information. This material is then used in a section focusing on analysis through a specific question. The main purpose of this is to help to tighten up essay technique.

The second aim is to provide a comprehensive range of sources for each of the issues covered. The questions are of the type which appear on examination papers, and some have worked answers to demonstrate the techniques required.

The chapters may be approached in different ways. The background narratives can be read first to provide an overall perspective, followed by the analyses and then the sources. The alternative method is to work through all the components of each chapter before going on to the next.

ACKNOWLEDGEMENTS

The author and publishers would like to thank the following for permission to reproduce material:

Penguin Books Limited for extracts from *Searchlight on Spain* by the Duchess of Atholl (1938); Penguin, and the Peters Fraser and Dunlop Group Ltd for an extract from *A Moment of War* by Laurie Lee (1991); Faber and Faber Ltd for extracts from *The Spanish Cockpit* by Franz Borkenau (1937); Jonathan Cape Ltd for an extract from *For Whom the Bell Tolls* by Ernest Hemingway (English edition, 1941); Berg Publishers for *Poem on the Antiquity of Spain* by Agustín de Foxá, in *The Spanish Civil War: A Cultural and Historical Reader*, ed. Alun Kenwood (1993); the Left Book Club for *Spain in Revolt* by H. Gannes and T. Repard (1936) and *Spanish Testament* by A. Koestler (1937); Pimlico for *Blood of Spain* by R. Fraser (1979/94); Macmillan for *The Spanish Civil War* by P. Knight (1991); and the Victoria and Albert Museum Picture Library for Republican posters from the Spanish Civil War.

The author would also like to thank Dr Tim Rees of the University of Exeter for permission to use extracts from his translations of Manuel Azaña on *caciquismo* (1923), the Bishops' Pastoral Letter on the Constitution (1932) and the JAP Manifesto (1932); Mr. J.W.D. Trythall of the University of York for an extract from his translation of a speech by Manuel Azaña to the Republican Action Party (1931).

1

THE PRIMO DE RIVERA DICTATORSHIP AND THE FALL OF THE MONARCHY

BACKGROUND NARRATIVE

Nineteenth-century Spain was torn apart by two civil wars between rival claimants to the throne. An unstable and short-lived republic (February 1873–December 1874) gave way to a constitutional monarchy under Alfonso XII. The 1876 Constitution introduced a bicameral parliament and by 1890 universal male suffrage was established. But, if a new age of political enlightenment seemed at first to be dawning, it was not to be an age of gold: in the 'Disaster' year of 1898, the economically valuable Spanish colonies of Cuba, Puerto Rico and the Philippines were all lost to the United States.

Spain kept out of the First World War. Although neutrality brought economic prosperity, there also came inflation and internal conflict, including a general strike in 1917. In the same year, army officers, still blaming the politicians for the defeats of 1898, set up their own unions. On the far left, anarchism was growing fast. In the regions, there was serious unrest, notably Barcelona's 'Tragic Week' (1909), the 'Three Red Years' (*Trienio Bolchevique*) in Andalucía (1918–20), and guerrilla warfare in Catalonia during 1919–23 when 700 people were murdered. Worker against capitalist, Catholic against atheist, anarcho-syndicalist against conservative, regionalist against centralist, landless labourer against landowner showed divisions deepening in Spain. There were also divisions within the divisions. Captains of industry resented the hold on political power of the reactionary landowners. Landless labourers, already brutally repressed by the paramilitary Civil Guard, hated the conservative-minded small-holders, the Catholic favourites and potential allies of the landowners. 'Regenerationists', who looked to restore the greatness of Spain, deplored the corruption of local political bosses, known as *caciques*.

Deepening this chasm of national anxiety came the news in 1921 of a gruesome military defeat in Morocco. The reputation of the army top brass was pilloried in the subsequent report on the affair, and the King's role in the campaign was investigated by parliament. The Catholic Church felt threatened when the government seemed about to grant full public freedom of conscience in what church leaders saw as a gross act of state-sponsored atheism. Landowners felt undermined by government attempts at land reform. But, according to Paul Preston in his 1993 biography of Francisco Franco, the flashpoint for General Primo de Rivera's *coup d'état* in 1923 came at Málaga. It was here, the embarkation point for Spanish Morocco, that a non-commissioned officer was murdered. When the suspect, a corporal, was pardoned by the King under political pressure, the officer corps felt doubly humiliated. The corrupt state had to be seized.

Primo de Rivera's dictatorship lasted seven years. Its politics reflected both reactionary and progressive attitudes, but eventually Rivera alienated as broad a political spectrum as had supported him in 1923. In January 1930 he withdrew from politics to exile in Paris, where he died. His successor, General Berenguer, headed a divided government. Although he restored political parties, as well as the four local administrations of Catalonia, parliament (the Cortes) was to be delayed until spring 1931. Berenguer's rule was not a smooth 'transition in reverse' to the system before Rivera's coup, but nor could it be a gradualist transition forward, given the level of support for more radical change, even a new dictatorship. The relatively free municipal elections of April 1931 were in effect a referendum on the monarchy, and they showed overwhelming support for the Republicans and Socialists. Alfonso XIII stepped down and the Second Republic was born.

ANALYSIS (1): WHAT DID THE DICTATORSHIP OF PRIMO DE RIVERA ACHIEVE?

When, in September 1923, as Captain-General of Barcelona, General Miguel Primo de Rivera issued a *pronunciamiento* overturning the Liberal government of García Prieto, he was seen by many as an almost messianic figure, leading a crusade against political corruption, social chaos and imperial humiliation. He was backed by the King, the army, the Church and a wide popular consensus. Yet, although his period of rule to January 1930 is called the *Dictadura*, his was not a dictatorship that followed rigid lines of policy. In Spanish Morocco, he moved from a policy of withdrawal to a strategy of war and consolidation. Initially he seemed keen to maintain an army promotions system based strictly on seniority, but he came to favour advancement through merit. He appeared to be sympathetic to the ambitions of moderate Catalan regionalism, but soon moved to a distinctly unsympathetic centralism. He planned for a constituent Cortes but then abandoned the idea.

Although, as Hugh Thomas has noted, Rivera's regime lacked the organized mass base and fanatical imperialism that might have labelled it fascist,[1] the 'Dictator' nevertheless dismissed the pre-existing Cortes, suspended elections and trial by jury, presided over a highly regulated education system, censored the press and forced many people, including some conservatives, into exile. On the other hand, Rivera was also in many ways a humane figure, concerned to alleviate the grinding poverty in which much of Spain's population lived. He posted military delegates to each region as 'pocket iron surgeons', to excise corruption. Sadly, their attempt to free the electorate from the hold of the *caciques* was no more than a qualified success.

The same could be said of Rivera's attempt to build a wide body of political support. Even after the end of the war in Morocco in 1926, when he felt able to 'liberalize' his regime, he never managed to persuade even the moderate Socialists to join his National Assembly. Rivera's Unión Patriótica (UP), which he hoped would give his regime a façade of public zeal, was a failure. His dynamic economic programme was open to political sabotage and susceptible to fluctuations in the world economy. Although Rivera banned the anarcho-syndicalist trade union, the CNT, and secured the cooperation of the moderate Socialist trade union, the UGT, he was never able to ensure united and consistent left-wing support. Three years later, in 1927, banned anarchists secretly re-established themselves as the small underground attack group, the Iberian Anarchist Federation (FAI).

In Catalonia and the Basque Country Rivera at first pursued a genuinely open-minded policy, in the hope that granting a regional assembly to Catalonia would uphold the authority of his Catalan conservative allies in the Lliga (Catalan Regionalist League). It did not, and Rivera saw no alternative but to abolish the assembly, much to the delight of his centralist supporters. As a result, the political tide in Catalonia, further strengthened by Rivera's banning of the Catalan flag, flowed instead towards the more radical anti-clerical Catalan separatism and republicanism as embodied in the Esquerra (Catalan Left Coalition). In the Basque Country, too, Rivera abandoned his original plans for a measure of regional autonomy under pressure from his military associates. However, he retained conservative Basque officials in their posts, while, as S. Payne has shown, the tariff on imported goods and state subsidies to local industry greatly assisted the economy of the Basque Country and, by extension, that of Spain.[2]

Rivera's social policies show similar contrasts. The government's policy on the publication of books in Catalan and Basque was tolerant. Basque culture flourished. The regime built 2,000 new schools and refurbished 2,000 others, and prioritized technical training. At the same time, Rivera disciplined university professors who criticized his government and, in a highly controversial move, delighted the Church by recognizing degrees awarded by Catholic universities. This infuriated the liberal intelligentsia. Less controversial were cheap housing for workers and higher maternity benefits for women. On the other hand, women were still barred from voting.

Social and economic progress was essential to national regeneration, but Rivera was limited in his options and dependent both on a healthy international economy and on internal cooperation. A worthy scheme was stillborn in 1928 when the *latifundistas* (large landowners) resisted the introduction into the countryside of compulsory wages and conditions arbitration committees (*comites paritarios*) which were already operating successfully in urban areas. Similarly, José Calvo Sotelo, Rivera's finance minister, was blocked in his attempts to use tax increases to pay for public works, and had to resort to heavy borrowing and an 'extraordinary budget' which led, in 1928, to the collapse of the peseta. Raymond Carr has criticized Rivera's Council for National Economy for being too bureaucratic,[3] but at the time it seemed a sensible means of pursuing autarky, as did high tariffs and state subsidies to industry. The policy of granting monopolies led to Spanish dependence on the USSR for oil. Nor was there any let-up in industrial unrest. In 1924 the Asturian Mineworkers' Union called a general strike; it failed, and the employers imposed even longer working hours.

However, there were several areas of success. Apart from the successful urban arbitration committees, bold, imaginative public works schemes led for a time to near-full employment: new roads were built and old ones tarmacked; an extended railway network included the first trans-Pyrenees rail link between Spain and France; and 60–80 million pesetas per annum were allocated to hydro-electric schemes. Two international exhibitions in 1929 promoted tourism and Spain's image of national regeneration, celebrating Spanish achievement past and present: the Ibero-American Exposition in Seville and the Barcelona International Exhibition. The Catalan historian Albert Balcells has suggested that Rivera hoped, rather optimistically, that the Barcelona Exhibition would build a political bridge to regional sentiment in Catalonia.[4]

Gerald Brenan, in his pioneering work *The Spanish Labyrinth*, first published in 1943, pointed out that the upswing in the world economy assisted Spain's own development.[5] However, could Spain's prosperity last without a sustained rise in agricultural exports? Whatever happened internationally, domestic political consequences arising from Spain's economic performance were bound to follow. Historians have offered contrasting perspectives on this. Hugh Thomas, in his highly readable *The Spanish Civil War*, first published in 1961, juxtaposes people's high expectations, thanks to a new consumer culture, with the arrival of the economic slump in the late 1920s.[6] The resultant disillusionment was made even more painful given the Dictatorship's earlier impressive record of a 300 per cent increase in production and commerce. And even had there been no economic slump, Primo de Rivera had still failed to capitalize on the 'feel-good' factor to wed the people to a more lasting and up-to-date replacement for the monarchy.

Writing in the mid-1980s, an expert on the Rivera dictatorship, Shlomo Ben-Ami, drew attention to the political consequences of economic migration to towns and cities. This had been generated by the opportunities to work in public works schemes and expanding industry: in these more 'open' environments, relatively free of *caciquismo*, the migrant electorate became less deferential and more prone to support radical politics.[7] The American historian Gabriel Jackson, writing in 1959, stressed the positive legacy of the public works programme: it was a base for further modernization during the Republic (1931–6). Paul Preston, on the other hand, has drawn attention to the heavy burden bequeathed to the Republic by the Rivera dictatorship's excessive spending.[8]

Clearly, then, the economic history of 1920s Spain cannot be seen in isolation. Rivera's successes and failures need to be put into a wider historical and international perspective. His public works schemes built on the progress of previous governments, and were in turn expanded and coordinated by the Republic. The arbitration committees were anticipated in post-1918 legislation and were successfully introduced into rural areas in 1931.

On the negative side, the war against the Riff and Jabala rebels in Spanish Morocco was a severe drain on the economy and Spain's military manpower. However, Rivera's initial plan – withdrawal – was rejected scornfully by the army, so he went instead for the military option. With French help, the Spanish defeated the rebels and forced their leader, Abd-el-Krim, to surrender in 1926. Victory in Morocco was immensely popular at home, but it did not guarantee loyal or sustained support from the army. The policy of promotion through merit, which Rivera was determined to pursue, won him support from the officers in Spain's elite Army of Africa (Africanistas), but earned him the bitter enmity of the ultra-traditionalist artillery corps, who went on strike in 1926 and were involved in a coup attempt in 1928. For a time they were even disbanded. Rivera also undermined his own chances of gaining support from the army by failing to address grievances over low wages and obsolete weapons. His inability to get the army as a whole firmly on side proved fatal. The captains-general responded unenthusiastically to his 'back me or sack me' telegram of January 1930, and the King was able to use this 'unconstitutional' manoeuvre as a pretext for forcing Rivera to resign. Even so, some key elements within the army, notably the Africanistas, were still loyal to Rivera and appalled at King Alfonso's cynical 'dropping of the pilot'. Perhaps ironically, Rivera's very achievements in modernizing the country seemed to have made the monarchy an anachronism. But it was Rivera who fell first. 'Spain, One and Great!' had been the rallying cry of Rivera's UP, but if his rule showed anything, it was that Spain could not unite around a slogan, however inspiring.

Questions

1. Was Primo de Rivera a weak dictator?
2. What did Spain gain from Primo de Rivera's dictatorship?

ANALYSIS (2): WHAT WAS THE SIGNIFICANCE OF THE FALL OF THE MONARCHY IN 1931?

Four days after the municipal elections of April 1931, and two days after the provisional government inaugurated the Second Republic,

King Alfonso XIII published his farewell message. This manifesto for the past and future raises several questions about his own role in politics, the position of the monarchy, and the wider nature of Spanish politics. For example, the results of the municipal elections did indeed, as Alfonso maintained, show public alienation from the monarchy, but this was not universal. The King had made mistakes, as he recognized, but was it 'without malice', as he claimed? People would, he continued, come to appreciate his consistent efforts to serve Spain to the best of his abilities. But to be a monarchist was not necessarily to be loyal to Alfonso as an individual: many monarchists were deeply disillusioned with him. The King's prerogatives were, he said, historical and national rather than personal to himself: but he had become closely identified with political controversy. Standing in the way of the national will would risk civil war, he declared, but the experience of the Republic would show that this national will was in fact divided against itself. He was 'King of all Spaniards'; but the Carlists (supporters of a rival branch of the royal dynasty) would hotly dispute that claim. Spain's destiny must be decided by Spain; but the Civil War would highlight the role other powers would play in deciding Spain's future. Alfonso declared he was suspending his royal powers while the nation decided his future: he hoped (in vain) to be recalled to the throne.

The historical significance of Alfonso's decision is twofold: it helps demonstrate the spread of republican and anti-monarchist sentiment in Spain by 1931, and it provides a basis for tracing the development of monarchist resistance to the Republic. Raymond Carr writes of Alfonso's 'moral isolation' in 1931,[9] yet the King's moral authority had been shrinking for decades. He saw himself as a stabilizing factor in a very fluid political situation that featured competing cliques and changing alignments, in which he was sure to offend one faction or another. In the early 1920s he was accused of employing divide-and-rule tactics, which further damaged an already divided Conservative Party. As a 'hands-on' monarch, Alfonso was, as Carr points out, inevitably identified with unpopular government decisions, such as the sending of working-class Spaniards to shore up mining concerns in Morocco. The King's image also suffered badly from the bloody defeat at Annual (1921).

Perhaps not surprisingly, Spain's long tradition of republicanism came to a head in the 1920s. The Annual affair produced a radical anti-monarchist alliance in 1926, and republicanism was fed further in 1928 by state recognition of Catholic university degrees. During demonstrations against the policy, the King's statue at Madrid University was vandalized beyond repair. It is a sign of how unpopular the King had become by 1928 that the leader of an abortive revolt against him was a leading conservative monarchist politician, Sánchez Guerra. Despite his failure, or perhaps because of it, Guerra became something of a national hero for his opposition to the King. Monarchists and republicans alike were demanding a decision-making Cortes. Guerra himself remarked, 'I am not a republican, but I recognize that Spain has a right to be a republic.'

The Pact of San Sebastián (August 1930) has been described by the Spanish historian Juan Pablo Fusi as 'the central event in the opposition to the monarchy of Alfonso XIII'.[10] Under this pact, Spanish and Catalan republicans agreed to work together in exchange for a guarantee of Catalan autonomy; it further underlined the impossibility of the King's task of convincing the political elite to operate on his terms. The pact was supported by figures as diverse as Azaña, a progressive Republican; Alcalá Zamora, a conservative Liberal converted to republicanism by his disillusionment with the King; Lerroux, a right-wing Radical; Maura, a Conservative; and de los Rios, a Socialist intellectual. It also enjoyed the support of army radicals.

The King's unpopularity helped boost military involvement in republicanism. In 1930 junior officers staged a revolt at Jaca in Aragón. Many of the military had a personal grudge against the King because he had not kept his promise to overturn Rivera's policy on promotion through merit and the dictator's harsh policy towards the artillery corps. However, the Jaca Revolt failed to spark off a wider uprising, and collapsed: its two leaders were shot for treason. But the political shockwaves from these peacetime executions dwarfed even the trial of Sánchez Guerra. The two young officers became martyrs to an ever more popular republican cause.

Gerald Brenan observed that 'No king or dictator could hope to hold Spain if the towns were against him.'[11] Yet that was exactly Alfonso's position in early 1931. Madrid and most provincial cities voted overwhelmingly Republican or Socialist, with a turnout twice the normal size, in the municipal elections. These damaging results presented Alfonso with something of a *fait accompli*. The Minister of War, General Berenguer (who had recently been Prime Minister), and General Sanjurjo, Commander of the Civil Guard, advised Alfonso that all was lost. By then, for most people in the upper and middle classes, a republic seemed preferable to Bolshevism: at least if Alfonso gave way to a presidency, Spain would not risk becoming the world's second proletarian state.

If the King played a central role in uniting his various opponents in opposition to himself, if not to the monarchy, he played a less central role in the development of monarchist opposition to the Republic. As his Farewell Message suggested, his initial reaction was realistic: to let the Republic be. But when the new government seized his property, exiled him for life and launched a ferocious attack on the Church and the very national order he had left office to defend, he became more amenable to the overtures of monarchist cliques. While the Church praised the monarchy as an institution, and Alfonso as King, other monarchist groups were mobilizing. They fell into two camps, the Alfonsists and the Carlists, each loyal to one of two rival lines within the Borbón dynasty. They all despised the 'atheistic' Republic; the Carlists also saw the chance to reassert themselves after their defeats at the hands of the Alfonsists during the nineteenth-century Carlist Wars. Some monarchists favoured a constitutionalist approach, wearing the Republic down from within. However, the higher-profile elements were more militant, pursuing a doctrine of 'catastrophism' – that is, violent and liberating convulsion which would bring the Republic crashing down and lead to the restoration of the monarchy.

It is important to realize that Alfonsists and Carlists were rivals: indeed, Carlists saw Alfonsine rule as iniquitous. Yet to a significant extent they cooperated. Both were militant, and bitterly critical of such right-wing 'moderates' as José María Gil Robles; but when the occasion demanded they were prepared to work with these same moderates, notably at election time. The government's 'revolutionary' reform policies made the monarchists increasingly sceptical of the constitutionalist approach, and in 1932 they formed the 'catastrophist' political parties, Comunión Tradicionalista for the Carlists (hence, 'Traditionalists') and Renovación Española for the Alfonsists. Both parties also operated as extra-parliamentary groups, hatching plots to destroy the Republic. The catastrophists relished their romantic struggle on the periphery of Spanish politics. Renovación Española plotted with military die-hards and sent delegates to lobby the Duce and the Pope. In the Carlist camp, paramilitary units (requetés) drilled for the coming conflict, supported by militant Catholic priests and, for historian Martin Blinkhorn, resembling Mussolini's squadristi.[12]

Hugh Thomas has noted that although Alfonso requested that nothing stand in the path of democracy in April 1931, during the Civil War he was active politically while resident in Italy: he gave generous financial help to the Nationalists and used his influence with the Italian state. Thomas also points up the class differences between Alfonsists, among whom wealthy landowners and financiers were prominent, and Carlists, who comprised less affluent aristocrats, peasants, skilled craftsmen and shopkeepers disillusioned by the government's economic agenda.[13]

Writing in the mid-1990s, George Esenwein and Adrian Shubert's emphasis is rather on the way Alfonso XIII himself betrayed the constitutional monarchy by accepting Primo de Rivera's coup and his *Dictadura*.[14] Predictably, this boosted the Republican cause as shown by the conversion of Alcalá Zamora, later President of the Republic. Esenwein and Shubert also offer a different perspective from Thomas's on the division between Alfonsism and Carlism: that the Alfonsine Renovación Española was not a mass party like the Carlist Comunión Tradicionalista but·that it nevertheless wielded considerable economic influence and had close associates in the army. For Carr, however, it was the Carlists who were 'the most serious and consistent plotters', though he, too, stresses the strong connection between generals in the Civil War and Alfonsists.[15] The consensus is that, at grassroots level, it was the Carlist *requetés* who played a crucial role on the Nationalist side, providing some of Franco's most highly trained and fanatical soldiers. Indeed, the Carlists had come to regard Gil Robles's 'accidentalism' as anathema, far too moderate for their apocalyptic tastes.

Brenan also allows Alfonso the attempt to return to constitutional government in 1930 – without the risk of elections – but stresses that leading politicians would not cooperate. On the contrary, their anti-monarchist, pro-republican stance acquired its highest profile yet in the August 1930 Pact of San Sebastián.[16] Carr's rather different emphasis is on General Berenguer's role in delaying the elections, which added fuel to the campaign against the King. And the one party that in 1930 was monarchist – the Unión Monárquica Nacional – was at odds with Alfonso over his dismissal of General Primo.

In the end, the monarchists' uncompromisingly independent stance could not be sustained. In any case, the Civil War's most celebrated Nationalist leader, Francisco Franco, did not like the idea of working with independent-minded paramilitary groups, whether monarchist or fascist. He therefore subsumed them all in a 'super-movement', the Spanish Traditionalist Phalanx of the Groups of the National Syndicalist Offensive (FET y de las JONS), where they could be more easily controlled. Alfonso XIII did not formally abdicate until 1941, and for loyal Alfonsists he remained a symbol of hope; Franco, on the other hand, had no intention of undermining his own supremacy by restoring the King. It would be forty-four years after Alfonso's departure before the monarchy would be restored in the person of his grandson, King Juan Carlos. No Carlist pretender has challenged him. Yet.

Questions

1. How did the monarchy contribute to the growth of republicanism during the period 1921–31?
2. How important was monarchism in the Second Republic and the Civil War?

SOURCES

1. THE PRIMO DE RIVERA DICTATORSHIP IN CONTEXT

Source A: Manuel Azaña on the power of the *cacique*, 1923.

The oligarchy, as a system, and *caciquismo* as an instrument – the exclusion of the will of the rest – derive from before the constitutional regime and the suffrage and have persisted with them . . . The *cacique* scandalizes us because the public conscience is more sensitive than fifty years ago . . . The blackest side of the activities of the *cacique* is the everyday sordid oppression, that rarely gets reported in the press or in parliament; an oppression that bears fruit in votes, because it demands them . . . The kingdom of the *cacique* rests fundamentally on two bases: economic and professional. The ownership of the land; a little – or a lot – of disposable income, and the offer of some necessary services, such as medical help, are the strongest means of hitching the people to his wagon . . . That which the loanshark or the doctor does not take for himself is fruit left to the priest, because (heavens above!) here also the true evangelicals are few and far between . . . The serious combat against the *cacique* is sustained by the organizations of landworkers and small peasants . . . [These] germs of peasant democracy are destroying the political bands and unmasking the allies of the *cacique*.

Source B: a Left Book Club viewpoint, 1936.

In the summer of 1922, the report of the committee, headed by General Picasso, was presented. Promptly the Council of Ministers suppressed it . . . Among the punishments recommended for the culpable was death for the high commanding generals in Morocco and several of the ministers in Madrid . . . A storm of protest burst over the news that the Picasso report was to be shelved. The King dissolved Parliament. New elections left conditions unchanged. The way was open for a dictator to step in . . . With an iron hand [Primo de Rivera] put an end to the movement which threatened to implicate the King himself. The nobility, the large landowners, the Church dignitaries, the monarchist pensioned mayors, the responsible militarists, all breathed a sigh of relief at the advent of the Primo de Rivera dictatorship.

Source C: Franz Borkenau, an Austrian sociologist, on the achievements and problems of the dictatorship.

What elements of modern European life there are to-day [1937] in Spain mostly date from the time of Primo; *the republicans are loath to acknowledge it.* But wherever there is a splendid road (and there are many), a modern inn in a small town, a new breakwater at some important port, a modern barrack or a modern prison, in nine out of ten cases it will have been constructed under Primo's administration. The dictatorship was able to secure the foreign loans needed for this work of construction. And at first it had the enthusiastic support of the industrial bourgeoisie . . . Neither was the dictator unaware of the need for giving the urban proletariat something more than prisons and cartridges in order to make it cooperate. For the first time in Spanish history a constructive effort was made to solve the 'social problem'. Compulsory collective bargaining was introduced, in order to secure acceptable wages for workers . . . Altogether it was the greatest attempt ever made to transform Spain into a modern country . . . But . . . from the first to the last moment [Primo] was in power, he was passively tolerated . . . Moreover, Primo's regime was not only up against the profound Spanish apathy that confronts constructive effort; it contained within itself elements absolutely incompatible with the winning of mass support. A progressive dictatorship such as his must rely, in the first place, on the bourgeoisie and the progressive intelligentsia. But Primo had to foregather with their two natural enemies, the army and the Church.

Source D: a Right Book Club viewpoint, published in 1938.

Once he is stirred, the Spaniard is a crusader, but he does not readily understand a crusade against an enemy so amorphous as apathy. Though Primo de Rivera failed to get the Spaniard to appreciate collective civil responsibilities, so that it became increasingly difficult to lay aside his powers . . . his dictatorship did much good work in other directions . . . One of its great works was an attempt to assist labour towards a wise development, and Primo de Rivera instituted what were known as Comites Paritarios, composed of representatives of employers and employees . . . Largo Caballero, later seduced to the cause of the extremists, did great work in those years . . .

It is amusing to read in reputedly well-informed British periodicals that the Republic and its politicians had bestowed the inestimable boon of electric light upon the poor country villagers. The writers probably believe this, and are unaware that the credit for the initiative in most of the great hydro-electric schemes was due to the Dictatorship, whose schemes would have absorbed something like the total estimated national wealth . . . The Ministers of the Dictatorship were over-optimistic in their finance. That, perhaps, was the most important reason for the fall of the Dictator; for the over-expenditure resulted in conditions which gave the agitators their opportunity to pull down first the Dictatorship itself, and secondly the Monarchy . . . It was a strange, patriarchal sort of Dictatorship, one of the most moderate, when one considers the difficulties of governing this fierce nation.

Source E: an evaluation of the dictatorship by historian and MP Katharine Atholl, 1938.

For forty or fifty years Spain has had her Socialist and trade-union movements, by no means confined to the towns. A peasant rising, however, as recently as 1919 had been fruitless, and since Primo de Rivera's seizure of power in 1923, though some useful constructive work had been achieved, no agrarian reform had been possible. Moreover, there had been no freedom to ventilate grievances in speech or press, no free elections, and no Cortes with any powers to legislate; while the desire of Catalonia for autonomy had been sternly refused. Some universities had been suppressed; professors and teachers were miserably paid . . . and religious tests had been imposed on State officials. The dictatorship, in fact, by overriding the Constitution, had read the nation a lesson in anarchy.

Questions

1. Explain the references to: (a) 'the republicans are loath to acknowledge it' (Source C) (2); (b) 'a lesson in anarchy' (Source E). (2)
2. How revealing is Source B as to the nature of Spanish government in the early 1920s? (3)
3. What can be inferred from Sources A and E as to political and economic relationships in rural Spain in the 1920s? (4)
*4. Assess the relative value to historians of the evidence provided by Sources C and D. (6)
5. Using these sources and your own knowledge, comment on the description of Primo de Rivera's rule as 'one of the most moderate' types of dictatorship. (8)

Worked answer

*4. [Apart from considering the accuracy or otherwise of these sources, also give thought to language and tone and other senses in which the sources may or may not be 'reliable'.]

What Borkenau says in Source C about the lack of active support for the Rivera regime can to some extent be corroborated: the Unión Patriótica did not become the affirmative mass-movement he had hoped for, and the Socialist Party would not join the National Assembly. However, the Socialist Largo Caballero joined Rivera's Council of State, even though he later distanced himself from the regime. As Borkenau suggests, it is true that Rivera found it difficult to unite right and left behind him. On the other hand, Rivera was not the first to attempt to solve the 'social problem'. Earlier governments had both initiated public works schemes, which after all have a social and political as well as an economic function, and made efforts to arbitrate in labour disputes.

Both Borkenau and the authors of Source D make generalized assertions about Spanish 'apathy' in the face of 'constructive effort'. Contrary to the authors' claims, many thousands willingly sought work in the public works schemes. The Africanista infantry also had cause to appreciate Rivera and were shocked when he was dismissed.

Borkenau's language and tone are relatively detached, though his repetition of the word 'modern' suggests admiration. Despite the provenance of Source D, its assessment is not entirely one-sided. It is true that politics intrude more clearly ('a wise development . . . seduced to the cause of the extremists . . . gave the agitators their opportunity'). They are also not averse to stereotypes: witness their references to 'the Spaniard' and 'this fierce nation'. They are somewhat patronizing, for example towards sections of the British press, though that of itself does not make their specific point of criticism wrong. Although themselves right wing, they acknowledge Largo Caballero's 'constructive effort' in the field of labour relations, while criticizing the financial policy of the dictatorship. Both sources give useful near-contemporary insights into the achievements and problems of Rivera's rule. Neither can be dismissed as mere propaganda.

As always, it depends to some extent on what the historian is looking for; and what his or her source is 'valuable for'. For unleavened propaganda one would look further afield. Nevertheless, Right Book Club analyses provide a counterweight to analyses such as Sources B and C.

SOURCES

2. THE MONARCHY AND THE BIRTH OF THE SECOND REPUBLIC

Source F: Left Book Club authors on the events of 1930.

On August 17, 1930 republican leaders met at Hotel de Londres, San Sebastian. Headed by the extreme Right republican leaders, such as Niceto Alcala Zamora, later President of the 1931 Republic; Alejandro Lerroux, later associated with the fascist leader Jose Maria Gil Robles, Miguel Maura, and others, a pact was drawn up compromising whatever differences there were to attain the common object of the establishment of a republic. They counted on nation-wide general strikes and support of the bulk of the army.

Captain Fermin Galan, a heroic republican figure, author of an idealistic book for the regeneration of Spain, *The New Creation*, on December 12, 1930 led what was known as the Jaca Revolt.

The fact that Captain Galan commenced the revolt prematurely shows the mistrust of the republican officers towards the republican civil leaders, who constantly postponed the hour of revolution. Captain Galan and his associates hoped to confront the republican leaders with a *fait accompli* and thus compel them to act further. The revolt was a miserable failure. Together with Captain Angel Garcia Hernandez, Captain Galan was court-martialled and sentenced to death. At the trial he was asked: 'Did you have accomplices?' 'Yes,' was the reply. 'Who are they?' 'Yourselves, cowards!' shouted the condemned captain.

Source G: a pro-monarchy perspective.

The outstanding feature of the tragedy of the fall of the Monarchy was the statesmanship of Alfonso XIII. It would be hard to find a more patriotic and disinterested gesture than he made on the eve of his departure, when he issued his public proclamation . . .

'I prefer to stand resolutely aside rather than provoke a conflict which might array my fellow countrymen against one another in civil and patricidal strife . . .

'I shall await the true and full expression of the collective conscience and . . . I deliberately suspend my exercise of the Royal power and am leaving Spain, thus acknowledging that she is the sole mistress of her destinies. Also I now believe that I am fulfilling the duty which the love of my country dictates. I pray God that all other Spaniards may feel and fulfil their duty as sincerely as I do.'

Source H: Franz Borkenau on the April 1931 municipal elections.

The polls demonstrated . . . facts of primary importance for the future. The revolutionary movement had hardly yet reached the countryside; the peasant was untouched; which meant, after all, that it had no deep roots in Spain as a whole. The countryside still obeyed the *caziques* [*sic*] and the aristocrats and voted monarchist. But . . . with two or three exceptions, all the provincial capitals voted for the united list forwarded by the coalitions of those parties that had signed the pact of San Sebastian. The monarchy had been optimistic; the result came as a terrible shock. The results in Barcelona were decisive. There everybody had expected the success of the Lliga; the Esquerra came in with an overwhelming majority. A few hours later Maciá proclaimed the independent Catalan republic.

The only possible help lay in the military. But the generals saw no reason to defend Alphonso, whom they had learned to hate ... [The King] issued a pathetic proclamation that he resigned in order to spare the country civil war.

Source I: Minister of War Manuel Azaña speaking in July 1931.

A year ago today the forces that prepared and brought about the revolution had still not come to agreement. Three months ago the limping monarchy was still trying to aim its weapons against us. And three days ago, after the Spanish people had said let there be a republic and the Republic had been born [in April 1931], three days ago we went to the Constituent Cortes and told them: 'Here are the powers that the republican people delegated to us' ...

Some might wish to rub out the memory of December like a bad dream ... But it does not embarrass me at all, as a member of the government, in a difficult and sensitive post, it does not embarrass me at all to invoke the memory of the December revolution which was the starting point for the victorious vote of April. ('Hear, hear.' Loud applause.) The vote of April did no more than corroborate and sanction within the legality of the polls the effort and the propaganda of the martyrs for freedom of December, morally victorious if apparently defeated ...

And I say here, friends and co-religionists, from my sensitive position of power that this memory does not embarrass me at all, because I have always and still do maintain that against tyranny everything is permissible and no law is binding. Just as I maintain that against the revolution that has now become the Republic by sanction of popular elections nothing is permissible that steps outside legal channels. (Long and loud applause.)

Questions

*1. Explain the references to: (a) 'and others' (Source F); (b) 'in a difficult and sensitive post' (Source I). (2)
2. What grounds might the monarchy have had for being 'optimistic' (Source H)? (3)
3. Contrast the perspectives offered on the Jaca Revolt by Sources F and I. (4)
4. What are the underlying purposes of the July 1931 speech delivered by Azaña to the Republican Action Party? (6)
5. Critically examining these sources and using your own knowledge, discuss the circumstances which led to the transition from monarchy to republic. (8)

Worked answer

*1. [Two marks for each part means that you must also offer some analytical comment.]

(a) There are names omitted here: for example, Azaña, the Left Republican leader; de los Rios, the Socialist; and Mallol, the Catalan nationalist. The reason might be that Gannes and Repard, Marxists writing in 1936, were keen not to associate the political left overtly with the origins of the problem-plagued Second Republic. Hence the anonymous 'and others'.

(b) Azaña was Minister of War in the first government of the Second Republic. However, he was a Left Republican, critical of much of the Spanish army's record and its organization. As Minister of War he would be expected to work for the improvement of the armed forces, but *his* definition of the national interest would bring him up against army traditionalists.

2

THE SECOND REPUBLIC

BACKGROUND NARRATIVE

Spain's Second Republic was born, and survived, in discouraging international circumstances: the Great Depression corroding Europe's economies and societies; Hitler extinguishing Weimar pluralism and challenging the European status quo; a brutal 'revolution from above' in the USSR; and, in Mussolini's Italy, a corporate state which bound together workers and managers, ostensibly for the national good. To many in Spain, such developments were healthy, a precedent to be followed.

The results of municipal elections on 12 April 1931 showed that Rivera's successors had failed to reconcile the populace to the monarchist regime. The King left Spain, and a provisional government took power. The politics of the Second Republic functioned – or sought to function – within a dysfunctionally broad spectrum of attitudes and agendas. From anticlerical Socialist Party to dogmatically clerical CEDA; from Catalan separatism to the mystical centralism of the Falange; from Alfonsine monarchists to Marxist POUM; and from conservative army officers committed to restoring the old state to anarchists frustrated by the new.

The Republic's political relations are explained partly by the results of the three general elections that took place during its lifetime. The first, in June 1931, elected a Cortes which drew up a controversial constitution and continued the reforms begun in April. The November 1933 election ushered in governments who did all they could to turn the clock back. The third election (February 1936) brought to power a government that, though lacking Socialist ministers, set out to reverse the work of its right-wing predecessors.

The 'reformist years' of 1931–3 seemed a malevolent eternity to the opposition right. The governments of Alcalá Zamora and his successor Azaña launched a bold programme of legislation. Thus, the Catholic Church (only 20 per cent of Spaniards were practising Catholics) was disestablished under Article 26 and its state subsidy was to end in 1933. Freedom of belief and religious practice was guaranteed provided it did not offend public morals and although the Jesuits were to be dissolved, other religious orders could continue if they did not endanger the state. However, these orders were barred from undertaking economic activity or teaching, and Church schools were to close within a specific time limit. Thus, the traditional status of the Catholic Church was to end. Clerical conservative Spain was appalled, and the government itself was fractured: in October 1931 Prime Minister Alcalá Zamora and Minister of the Interior Maura – both conservative Catholics – resigned.

Controversy also stalked land legislation. By mid-1931 the Law of Municipal Boundaries protected rural workers against cheap imported labour; arbitration committees on wages and conditions and protection for tenants against arbitrary eviction were established. Predictably, irate landowners and their political allies saw this as a declaration of war, as they did the Law of Agricultural Reform which expropriated, without full compensation, the largest landowners' estates.

The 1931–3 governments also introduced army reforms, limited autonomy for Catalonia, universal suffrage at twenty-three, freedom from arbitrary imprisonment, legal divorce and the abolition of the death penalty. Other innovations included old-age pensions. Progress in hydro-electric power continued from the Primo de Rivera dictatorship. Barcelona University gained autonomy; a People's University was founded in Madrid where adults were taught by postgraduates. Official statistics from the Ministry of Information claimed that by the end of 1932 10,000 new primary schools had been built. Cultural 'missionaries' took theatre, cinema and fine art to the rural populace. But were these life-enhancing changes or, as conservatives saw them, a threat to corrupt morals?

Of these reforms, which would be targeted by the right-wing governments in power from November 1933 to February 1936? In the process of reversing earlier legislation, CEDA deputies in the Cortes under Gil Robles wielded powerful influence. Thus, the Jesuits could teach again, while state education spending was slashed. There were nearly 19,000 peasant evictions in Estremadura alone, and rural unemployment rose as labourers lost their job security. Trade unions faced assaults from the Ministry of the Interior, whereas amnesties were granted to anyone involved in the August 1932 coup attempt led by General Sanjurjo.

Beyond parliament and law-making, how did left and right behave towards each other? They provided fuel for the Republic's opponents: in May 1931 convents and churches were burned and catacombs desecrated. At Castilblanco near Badajoz (Estremadura) the corpses of civil guardsmen were brutally mutilated. In 1934 the anarchist leader Durruti called a general strike in Zaragoza and a nation-wide strike of labourers was organized by the Socialist land-workers' union, the FNTT.[1] For two weeks that October, Socialist miners took over parts of Asturias, including the capital Oviedo. As things deteriorated in 1936, Madrid was plagued by strikes.

On the political right, the most famous assault on the state before the military revolt of July 1936 was the abortive putsch by General Sanjurjo and his followers in August 1932. A reaction against the Catalan Autonomy Bill and Agrarian Reform Bill, the 'Sanjurjada' failed in its primary goal of seizing power. However, the army learned much from this debacle. Meanwhile, in rural districts landlords resorted to subversion on a grand scale – refusing to allow cultivation and thus putting labourers out of work, and taking advantage of loosely drafted legislation. In turn, many reformers – notably Largo Caballero as Minister of Labour, 1931–3 – lost faith in the power of democracy to enact change effectively.

Versions of democracy survived, nevertheless, through eight years of peace and war. And, during the peacetime Republic, the artist Miró, poet and playwright Lorca and film director Buñuel led a flourishing world of culture. Women gained new prominence in journalism, trade union leadership and politics; the suffragist Victoria Kent became the Republic's first Director-General of Prisons.[2] And in parts of Spain there was a fundamental left-wing social, economic and political revolution – though it took civil war both to achieve it and to destroy it.

ANALYSIS (1): WHY, DESPITE ITS ACHIEVEMENTS, DID THE SECOND REPUBLIC PROVE SO UNSTABLE?

Between its birth in April 1931 and March 1939 when its last Prime Minister, Juan Negrín, fell from power, the Second Republic experienced fifteen changes of government. This in itself, however, says nothing specific of individual government tenure, one criterion for 'stability'. Azaña's first stint as Prime Minister, from October 1931, lasted nearly two years; at the other extreme, in July 1936 the government of Martínez Barrio survived for barely twelve hours. Of the eleven peacetime governments, eight lasted for six months or less. Add to this the political, social and economic 'wars' already being waged by interest groups all over Spain against these governments (let alone each other) by strikes, propaganda, obstruction and insurrection, and it may seem remarkable not only that anything significant was achieved but that civil war was delayed for so long. At times, Spain seemed locked into a vortex of instability.

The nature of the Republic's achievements was bound to inflame or frustrate: is it therefore more apt to say that it was because of these achievements, rather than despite them, that the Republic was so unstable? Tension between Barcelona and Madrid after the Catalan Autonomy Bill (1932) was due partly to the fact that the Catalan signatories of the 1930 Pact of San Sebastián saw the Bill as too diluted. Historians such as Albert Balcells and Norman Jones have noted the dramatic shift from 'tension' to 'crisis' in the autumn of 1934: inhaling the pure oxygen of Spain's 'October Revolution', Lluis Companys, head of the Catalan Republican Left Party and of the Barcelona regional government, now proclaimed a 'Catalan State within a Spanish Federal Republic'. For this initiative he was sentenced to thirty years in prison; the central authorities suspended the Catalan government (Generalitat), along with the autonomy law itself.[3]

In a democratic environment, what does political stability require? More than an origin based on consensus, which in April 1931 the Republic seemed superficially to have, it needs even-handedness and political subtlety. But these, unlike anxiety and disillusionment, were in short supply. For every newspaper banned, there was an inflammatory speech in the Cortes or at a party rally; for every politician imprisoned, an intimidating parade or debilitating strike. In turn, state attempts to restore equilibrium by force were often counter-productive. Indeed, the theme of provocation is woven throughout the Second Republic. There was readiness to provoke and to be provoked. When, in October 1934, ministers from the Spanish Confederation of Autonomous Rightist

Groups (CEDA) joined Lerroux's government, 'the Socialists [took] the bait and launched a hopeless assault on the state',[4] the most dramatic example being the Asturias Rising and subsequent commune which held out for two weeks before being crushed.

If a measure of instability is evident in all political systems, what made the Spanish example so extreme? Analysis of the period 1931–6 alone cannot provide the whole answer. After all, the 1931–3 governments' *raison d'être* was to challenge the pre-1931 order through legislation; the preoccupation of the right-wing governments of November 1933–February 1936 was to restore tradition and conserve it. Moreover, Frances Lannon's close analysis of the experience of the Catholic Church has shown that it already felt deeply insecure before the *annus horribilis* of 1931: would the demonic Republic now deal the final blow?[5] Similarly, landowners had long faced agitation from landless labourers: now, there was an additional scapegoat in the 'destructive Republic'.

The self-interest and self-image of groups and institutions were not only hurt by single-issue reforms aimed by the state directly at them. For example, the army was also antagonistic towards Catalan autonomy because it would destroy the unity of the *Patria*. Similarly, the Church was deeply anxious about land reform and the new politics: CEDA, the Church's political wing, described the 'atheistic' Republic as a communist class dictatorship hostile to the family, private property and the free market.

When centrifugal forces were at work concurrently, then chronic instability would follow. In 1933–4 both CEDA on the right and disillusioned Socialists on the left, led by Largo Caballero, were becoming more anti-constitutional in outlook. For the left this process had already begun in 1931, when its more radical elements felt that their idealized 'new Spain' was being sold out to compromise. The right countered with accusations that the old Spain was being subverted by revolutionary reform. Indeed, much venom was spat at the governments of the Second Republic: that they were more like pressure groups than governments, that their leaders were agitators not statesmen, that their law-enforcement was lawless and that they were led by their followers. And however decisively governments introduced reform, or reneged on it or repealed it, outcry was certain: from those who sought *more* change (Socialist, Communist or anarchist) and those who wanted no progressive legislation at all – army, Church and landowners, great and small.

Paul Preston's detailed research into the contemporary press has shown how newspapers and periodicals played a significant part in entrenching these positions. The press sustained an intoxicating aura of confrontation, while contributing to the making of revolution and reaction more directly. For example, left-wing papers conducted influential campaigns. One of these led in March 1934 to the forging of an Asturian Workers' Alliance which went on to organize the Asturias Rising. On the right, in a contagious spirit of 'catastrophism', the pro-CEDA Catholic daily *El Debate* intoned in January 1936, 'Between the ruin and the salvation of Spain there is no middle way.'[6] Newspapers were joined in the vanguard of protest by Spanish youth, who themselves had their own political press. Prominent in the Asturias Rising of October 1934 was the Socialist Youth Movement (FJS). On the extreme right, young Falangists led death-raids against the left – notably the murder of an Assault Guards officer in July 1936, in reprisal for which the right's new hero, José Calvo Sotelo, was assassinated.

A dense matrix of instability characterized the Second Spanish Republic, the political momentum veering towards the extremes – within governments such as those of Lerroux; within parties, for example, the Spanish Socialist Party (PSOE); and within movements, notably the anarchist National Confederation of Labour (CNT). High-profile operators like Largo Caballero and Gil Robles lost faith in the legal path, a route already despised by Alfonsist and Carlist monarchists and the Falange Española, the millennarian fascist movement of the *new* right.

To conclude: in the period 1931–6, legislation (and the dread of it) reacted with privilege and deprivation, exacerbating pre-existing tensions and leading ultimately to civil war. Speaking metaphorically, the Republic in 1931 had defined itself as an engine of change but it ignored a series of red lights and was derailed. Governments seemed at times less interested in building political bridges than in blowing them up. From late July 1936, the politics of the feud became the tactics and strategies of armies, and a plethora of conflicts now reduced themselves to a definitive formula: the open society versus its enemies. Analysis (2) seeks to consider why hopes of coexistence between Spanish people were dashed. However, as this first analysis has tried to argue, in the crisis atmosphere of the Republic hopes of coexistence were always fragile, and more or less unacceptable: to policy-makers and opinion-formers, to die-hard property-owners and to those they regarded as put on earth to serve them.

Questions

1. How significant was regional identity during the period 1931–6?
2. 'The events of October 1934 were of decisive importance in the history of the Second Republic.' Discuss.

ANALYSIS (2): WHY WERE HOPES OF COEXISTENCE BETWEEN THE SPANISH PEOPLE DASHED AFTER FEBRUARY 1936?

This analysis will focus on the fourteen months from May 1935 to July 1936. In order to place the February 1936 elections in perspective, some reference to the upheavals of October 1934 will be made. As will be seen, within a broad definition of 'coexistence', difficulties were to be experienced at all levels. Though there were always constraints and opportunities that prevented total fragmentation, this is not how it appeared to many at the time.

Already in October 1934 three CEDA ministers had been appointed to government, sparking working-class and regionalist revolts. Then, in May 1935, Prime Minister Lerroux reshuffled his cabinet, adding two more CEDA ministers: the CEDA leader Gil Robles became Minister of War. Together, this dissonant quintet would ensure the failure of coexistence in Spain. To call them 'Lerroux's ministers' rather misses the point. At the War Ministry, Gil Robles – pausing on his own resolute ascent to the summit – appointed a triad of generals to key posts, although Franco (Chief of General Staff) was more prepared at this stage to coexist with the Republic than were Fanjul (Under-Secretary of War) and Goded (Inspector-General and Director of the Air Force).

Gil Robles himself expected to succeed Prime Minister Lerroux's own successor Chapaprieta, who resigned over a budget crisis at the end of 1935. But the CEDA leader miscalculated: his glowing references to the death of parliamentary democracy, along with the yells of his youth wing (JAP) for 'All power to the chief!', merely alienated President Alcalá Zamora, who did not appoint him. Yet Gil Robles still had the power to sustain heavy CEDA pressure in parliament, and in the February 1936 election campaign he exhorted JAP to spread propaganda against the Republic.

Much to Gil Robles's fury, however, the right lost the February 1936 elections to the 'odious' Popular Front: a bitterly controversial result whose statistics have been analysed in depth by the Spanish historian Xavier Tusell Gómez. Following the Popular Front victory, more radical right-wingers, notably José Calvo Sotelo, began to dig a deeper furrow in Spanish politics.[7] Would Gil Robles now 'coexist' with such elements on the far right, or would he actively encourage his followers to join them? The view that the 'legal' path had failed was spreading, and Gil Robles could not obstruct the accelerating climb of far-right anti-parliamentary groups. Nevertheless, as Paul Preston has written, 'he played an active, and indeed crucial, role, in parliament and the press, in creating the atmosphere which made a military rising appear to the middle classes as the only alternative to catastrophe'.[8] Gil Robles used parliament for propaganda, but meaningful coexistence with the state was as unacceptable to him as it was to the militant Socialist Largo Caballero.

In jail after the October 1934 risings, and following his release at the end of 1935, Largo Caballero mused on Marx and revolution. But until the defeat of the right in the February 1936 elections he was prepared to coexist with Prieto, his reformist rival in the PSOE. Prieto's ambition to mobilize a broad front behind the Republic with a moderate reform agenda (what became the January 1936 Popular Front programme) won wide public support, reflected in the Popular Front victory. However, Largo Caballero was committed to his own root-and-branch plan to radicalize the PSOE with Communist Party support and now ended his tactical alliance with Prieto: he vetoed the idea of power-sharing by the PSOE, and his newspaper *Claridad* showed that his tolerance of the government was heavily qualified:

> We will not renounce our own right to criticize in order to maintain the vigilance of the working class, which is now marching forward to the final goal of our class, and, at the slightest sign of weakening, to set the working class against its present allies.[9]

Meanwhile, in the rural districts, people were coexisting less with each other than with trauma, confrontation and murder. Left provoked right, and vice versa. Churches and right-wing HQs in Córdoba province suffered incendiary attacks by the CNT. Forcing thousands out of work, landlords flooded arable land and faced the wrath of the FNTT. In the years of reaction (November 1933–February 1936), governments and landlords had driven through progress in reverse. Now the new Popular Front government was set on moving politics and society forward once more – but, just as surely, enraged their opponents when they reinstated forward-looking laws.

The role of the press, discussed in Analysis (1), underlines the limitations of coexistence within right-wing politics. *El Debate* lionized the Falange's mauling of the left, but the Falange scorned this praise, and frequently disrupted CEDA meetings. These were times of shifting loyalties and identities, with agents provocateurs adding to the confusion.

As Gerald Brenan explained in *The Spanish Labyrinth* the limits of coexistence were also evident at the level of 'high' politics. For example, President Alcalá Zamora was in the firing line from his prime minister, Azaña, who was bitterly resentful at Zamora's 'meddling' and his wish to dissolve the Cortes. But, if President Zamora and Prime Minister Azaña could not coexist, who would take the President's place were he to be impeached for this 'interference'? Ironically, it would be Azaña who now found himself head of state – on 10 May 1936, the fifth anniversary of the first church-burnings.[10] Who would become Prime Minister now that Azaña was President? The Left Republican whom Azaña chose, Casares Quiroga, seemed grudging in his attacks on left-wing violence. Neither Azaña nor Casares and his colleagues had the power to reconcile, inspire and unite. Increasingly, coexistence seemed confined to Casares's cabinet.

During the period May–July 1936, industrial relations hit rock bottom. Shipping, the hotel industry, and tram, railway and building companies all found themselves under economic siege. Employers undermined the arbitration committees and rejected the shorter working week reintroduced after the Popular Front election victory. Among workers' organizations, the anarchist CNT was 'coexisting' with neither the Socialist UGT (General Union of Workers) nor the Communist Party. And even if for the Communists and Largo Caballero's left wing of the Socialist Party revolution was a longer-term goal, their propaganda, along with the economic civil war, was enough, in the words of Paul Preston, 'to verify the exaggerated picture of unmitigated chaos being painted by Calvo Sotelo and Gil Robles'.[11] Moreover, although Prieto was gaining support within sections of the Socialist Party for his more centrist brand of politics, his meetings were attacked by the militant Socialist–Communist youth movement, the JSU – between its assaults on anarchists and Falangists. On this jagged edge of civilian politics coexistence was, for many, a forgotten cause.

There were exceptions to this rule. Catalonia, with its semi-autonomy restored, appeared relatively quiescent in the otherwise 'ominous'[12] spring of 1936. However, relentless headlines of bloody confrontation continued to sap national morale. For many months, with the political stakes so high, there had been no significant centre in Spanish politics. Disingenuously, Gil Robles blamed Spain's agony on the left. But whatever the hierarchy of causes for the impending national earthquake, it is not surprising that the army, or some of it, defender of eternal Spain's integrity, finally rose up. Those who sought to defend the new Spain, despite or because of the chaos of July 1936, resisted; in the final analysis, military could not coexist with military, either.

Questions

1. Why was the Second Republic not more successful?
2. What was the significance of Gil Robles and Largo Caballero in Spanish politics, 1931–6?

SOURCES

1. THE SOCIALISTS AND THE POPULAR FRONT

Source A: a Communist perspective from the Left Book Club, 1936.

Meanwhile the Madrid organisation of the Socialist Party, headed by Largo Caballero, had passed a resolution, to be introduced at the next Socialist national congress, urging organic unity with the Communist Party, and a serious split threatened within the Socialist leadership.

Indalecio Prieto, the right-wing Socialist leader, manoeuvred to oust Largo Caballero, who undoubtedly had the support of the majority of Socialists, as the events of the Civil War proved later. This alarming danger of a Socialist split, the tense situation created later on by fascist provocations in the great wave of strikes, and the clash between the anarcho-syndicalists and the united UGT were grist to the fascist mill.

Mundo Obrero, Communist official organ, worried over efforts of the fascists, Trotskyists, and some anarcho-syndicalists to rupture the People's Front, warned that under no circumstances must the united action of Left Republicans and the proletarian parties be broken.

Source B: from the reform manifesto of the left PSOE, led by Largo Caballero, March 1936.

We must put an end to the illusion that the proletarian socialist revolution can be brought about through the reform of present social conditions, i.e., that the transformation of private and corporate ownership of the means of production into common ownership by the whole society will result in the abolition of all classes and their fusion into a single community of workers. There is no other alternative but to destroy and rebuild society from its foundations ...

Step by step, the dictatorship of the proletariat ... will become a fully developed, classless democracy, in which State coercion gradually will disappear. The Socialist party will be the organ of such a dictatorship and will remain so for as long as the transition from one society to another may last, and for as long as the threats from the surrounding capitalist States may warrant the existence of a strong proletarian State ...

In order to accomplish this, it is essential to achieve the immediate unification of all revolutionary forces through the fusion, on the political and trade union fronts, of all workers' groups, and the complete divorce of the Socialist party from any reformist or centrist tendency.

Source C: Martínez Barrio, leader of the Republican Union Party, looks back at the problems of the Popular Front.

If the trade union movements or the Socialist and Communist parties disagreed with our point of view, why didn't they make it clear? Why did they agree to a pact whose fundamental aim was the consolidation of the Republican regime established in 1931 and of its constitutional charter?

Certain Socialists and all the Communists were suffering from the mirage of the Russian revolution of 1917, and handed us the dismal role of Kerensky. According to them, our mission was limited to smoothing their road to power, since the possibilities of the democratic revolution in the history of the Republic had been exhausted.

Source D: The pessimistic view of Gabriel Mario de Coca, a Prieto supporter.

I close my work with an impression of Bolshevist victory in every sector of the party. The Socialist parliamentary minority in the Cortes will be impregnated with a strong Leninist tone. Prieto will have few deputies on his side while Besteiro will be completely isolated as a Marxist dissenter . . .

The outlook that all this leaves for the future of the working class and of the nation could not be more pessimistic. The Bolshevist centipede dominates the proletariat's horizon and Marxist analysis indicates that it is on its way to another of its resounding victories. So that if in October 1934 it only achieved a short-lived Gil Robles government accompanied by the suspension of the constitution and the most horrible, sterile shedding of working class blood, it can now be expected to complete its definitive work in the future [cataclysm].

Source E: a very different perspective from Source A, by Katharine Atholl, 1938.

After the General Election of 1936 the Socialist and Communist youth organisations had united, and Caballero was working for a union of the two parties. But he was not a member of the Government, and his proposals for party fusion had been strongly opposed by the Socialist Right Wing, led by Señor Indalecio Prieto. Prieto's following steadily gained ground, and by June had secured a majority on [this] important issue. Whatever declarations, therefore, pointing to revolutionary aims, may have been made by Caballero at this time, it is important to remember that he spoke neither as a member of the Government nor even as leader of a united Socialist Party.

Questions

1. Explain the references to: (a) 'Trotskyists and some anarcho-syndicalists' (Source A); (b) 'Certain Socialists'; 'Kerensky' (Source C). (5)
*2. Using your own knowledge, and with reference to Sources B and E, explain why: (i) 'unification' was limited; (ii) the PSOE was unable to become 'the organ' of the dictatorship of the proletariat. (8)
3. How accurate do you find de Coca's assessment in Source D? (4)
4. Using these sources and your own knowledge, how far can it be said that the PSOE played an essentially detrimental role in the politics of the Republic, February–June 1936? (8)

Worked answer

*2. [For 2 (i), refer to specific contexts in which 'unity' was apparent, underlining its extent, limitations and impact. For 2 (ii), ensure you place the Socialist Party within the wider political arena and note the unforeseen development of September 1936, which was to find Largo Caballero – who seven months before had demanded such a 'dictatorship of the proletariat' – leading a 'united front' government against Franco's Nationalist rebels.]

2 (i). At the youth-movement level, the Socialist (PSOE) and Communist (PCE) parties did 'unite', as the JSU (United Socialist Youth), in April 1936. But this did not make for a complete meeting of minds. Indeed, pro-Prieto members of this new organization felt alienated: the Communist element had ousted the Socialist Party youth leaders in Madrid, and pro-Prieto meetings were disrupted by militant JSU hostile to the moderate Socialist leader. (Prieto sought cooperation with the Republican government.) At the trade union level, Socialists and Communists did 'unite'; so did the Socialist and Communist parties in Catalonia (late July 1936). This new United Socialist Party of Catalonia (PSUC) affiliated to the Communist Third International (Comintern). Nevertheless, elsewhere in Spain – notably in the north – the moderate Prieto wing of the Socialist Party remained strong, holding a majority on the party's national committee. 'Prietistas' rejected unification with the Communist Party, the cause embraced by Largo Caballero and his more radical Socialist supporters. Furthermore, Prieto attacked 'revolutionary euphoria' (Carr) as a red rag to fascism. Even so, the flawed but obsessive image of a 'communist threat' became more deeply embedded in the minds of the Republic's Nationalist enemies.

2 (ii). To achieve this, the Socialist Party (PSOE) would have needed to be in an effective position of power, which, for the time being, eluded it. It was in fact another Left Republican, Casares Quiroga, who succeeded Azaña as Prime Minister in May 1936. It is true that the now President Azaña had considered appointing Prieto to take his place as Prime Minister, but this had been blocked by Largo Caballero's militant faction of the PSOE. Despite this, Prieto was keen to build bridges to Casares Quiroga's government. Prieto's position was strengthened in June 1936 when more of his supporters were elected to the PSOE's national committee. These developments suggest that the PSOE did not fully accept the Marxist–Leninist 'dictatorship of the proletariat' which Largo Caballero was advocating at that time. In the wider political environment, other working-class movements had their own power bases and priorities, notably the CNT (anarchist) and POUM (Marxist, strong in Catalonia), while the Stalinist PCE (Communist Party) claimed 100,000 members by July 1936. In addition, the Republican government had itself been true to the spirit of reform. Ironically, in September 1936, the erstwhile 'Bolshevik' Largo Caballero became Prime Minister, his cabinet containing two Communists – and, from November, Prieto and four anarchists. In an anti-fascist war to defend democracy, the immediate 'dictatorship of the proletariat' was, from the government's perspective, irrelevant.

SOURCES

2. OPPOSITION TO THE LEFT, 1931–6

Source F: from the Bishops' Pastoral Letter on the Constitution (December 1931), published on 1 January 1932 in the Catholic newspaper *El Debate*.

Freedom for all associations, even the most subversive; and extreme precautions are taken to limit the religious congregations, which devote themselves to the most rigid perfection of their members, to social charity, to generous teaching and to the functions of the priesthood . . .

Notwithstanding, a distinction must be made between 'constituted power' and 'legislation' . . .

The acceptance of the constituted power does not imply in any way conformity, still less obedience, to legislation which is contrary to the law of God and of the Church. But nations are curable and legislation perfectable. So, without diminution or attenuation of the respect due to the constituted power, all

Catholics will consider it a religious and civic duty to display their zeal and to use all their influence to contain the ongoing abuses of legislation and to change for the better the unjust and damaging laws passed up to date.

Source G: from the Juventud de Acción Popular (JAP, the CEDA youth movement) Manifesto, October 1932.

As one of its postulates JAP still has faith in the legal struggle; but we advise the government that we are reaching the limits of its effectiveness: arbitrary suspension of the press, inhuman deportations, imprisonment . . . confiscations and the systematic persecution of the Church create a state of opinion whose consequences for the peace of Spain we would be the first to lament. Seeing that all avenues for legal action are closing, no other alternative remains but to exercise the right of legitimate defence . . .

Forget rebellion. In order to act against the government we shall move within legality; but in questions of . . . defence of our principles, not one step backwards. The Youth Movement wants to demonstrate that we live within Acción Popular's set of ideas, but also we declare that this attitude should not be taken by anybody as a sign of the cowardice of the right . . .

The Youth Movement does not now raise the question of the form of government. Not because we believe this to be a matter of no account, but because we estimate that the time has not yet arrived when this matter should be taken on board. We declare ourselves, therefore, partisans of the status quo. We do seek to not impose our viewpoint.

Source H: from *Spanish Testament* by Arthur Koestler, 1937.

All the protective legislation introduced by previous governments was repealed by the Gil Robles regime. The law rendering illegal the importation of non-local labour was repealed. The law with regard to lease-hold contracts was repealed, and more than 100,000 tenant farmers were given notice. The distribution of the land among the peasants was declared null and void . . . and the land was restored to its former owners, who let it lie fallow.

At the same time all unemployment relief was abolished, and the 873 million pesetas allocated to public works by the budget of 1933 was reduced in 1935 to 628 million.

The unrestrained tyranny of the feudal aristocracy was driving the Spanish economic system once more toward ruin. Whilst in most European countries a gradual recovery after the slump was discernible between 1933 and 1935, the curve of unemployment in Spain mounted steadily, reaching its peak in 1935 . . .

The masses had returned to their old state of unspeakable misery and suffering . . . This was the heritage which fell to the lot of the Spanish People's Front in February, 1936 . . .

From the very beginning, the defeated Spanish reaction concentrated all its efforts on making the world believe that Communism had come to power in Spain. It launched one of the most perfidious propaganda campaigns Europe has ever known – and one of the most successful.

Source I: from the National Front (Bloque Nacional) Manifesto, December 1935.

What we want is an old, time-honoured State with roots in the history of Spain. This State, which will respect all differences between individuals and provinces, must have the strength to extirpate the anti-national forces that, like a disease, threaten to sap the life of the Fatherland. Therefore, it must be an authoritarian, corporatist, and unifying State . . .

The new State will [restore] to all Spaniards peace and order. This task demands . . . the formation of a wide coalition of counterrevolutionary forces, acting on a well-defined platform . . . that will enable those elected to pursue with total unanimity the full implementation of its policies in parliament.

Such a platform must have as its foundation the replacement of the 1931 Constitution, whose legal status has already been undermined [deleted by censor], as well as the extirpation of Marxism, separatism, and laicism from national life.

Source J: José Calvo Sotelo speaks in the Cortes, 16 June 1936.

No more strikes, no more lock-outs, no more usurious interest, no more of capitalism's abusive financial formulae, no more starvation wages, no more political salaries gained by happy accident, no more anarchic liberty, no more criminal loss of production, for national production is above all classes, all parties, and all interests.

Many call that the fascist state. If it is, then I who share that idea . . . and believe in it, declare myself fascist.

Questions

1. What is meant by: (a) 'ongoing abuses of legislation' (Source F); (b) 'corporatist' (Source I)? (2)
2. (a) What can be inferred about Koestler's deep feelings in Source H? (3)
   (b) How would a member of the 'defeated Spanish reaction [right]' challenge Koestler's attempt to downplay the significance of communism? (4)
3. What questions would a historian wish to ask of Calvo Sotelo's claim to be 'fascist'? (Source J) (3)

*4. Comment on the value of Sources F and G for a historian studying opposition to the left, 1931–6. (6)

5. 'Opposition to the left during the period April 1931 to June 1936 became steadily more militant.' Discuss this view, using these sources and your own knowledge. (7)

Worked answer

*4. [Ensure you pick up on *attribution* (provenance) and that you confront the limitations as well as the benefits of these sources. This will require some knowledge of context.]

Source F presents an 'autobiographical' image of an insecure Church: one that feels itself not only besieged by anti-clerical legislation, but victimized by a biased constitution (paragraphs 1 and 2). It is clear that the bishops' stand on the Republic is 'accidentalist', desiring change from within: they exhort their readers to apply all possible pressure to have draconian laws repealed. The provenance tells us that the letter was published in *El Debate*. This provenance underlines lay Catholics' support for the bishops' denunciation of the Republic in 1931–2, a republic that, it is implied, is subverting traditional Spain and the religious means to uphold it. However, in this edited extract, the historian misses the full force of the bishops' attack, especially on secularist education policies. Moreover, it should not be assumed that all practising Catholics were anti-Republic. Conversely, Canon Albarrán condoned the notion of a violent uprising against the Republic, which makes Source F look positively restrained. Finally, it should be remembered that governments proved friendly to the Catholic Church between November 1933 and February 1936: to this extent, too, the evidence in Source F should be treated with caution.

Source G can be taken as an authoritative statement of JAP policy in the early years of the Republic. (Acción Popular had until April 1932 been known as Acción Nacional; from March 1933 it would be the keystone of CEDA.) Source G denounces what it sees as arbitrary and autocratic behaviour by Azaña's government and a partisan judiciary. But the tone is ambiguous and the historian would need to be alert to this. 'Forget rebellion' sounds 'accidentalist'; but 'all avenues for legal action are closing' suggests that a future assault on the Republican state *per se* cannot be ruled out. Thus, for the historian, Source G is a pointer to the JAP's latent 'catastrophism'. This is confirmed by later events: in 1935 JAP called for an authoritarian system and for Marxists and Freemasons to be wiped out; by the spring of 1936 it was marching *en masse* into the ranks of the Falange.

Finally, Sources F and G express only a corridor of views held by two groups and their supporters in 1932. For a fuller picture of opposition to the left during 1931–6 it would be necessary to consult evidence from, for example, such militant monarchists as Calvo Sotelo; the Falange; and anti-Republic factions within the armed forces.

3

THE MILITARY RISING

BACKGROUND NARRATIVE

Starting in 1931, a controversial agenda of military reform was pursued by War Minister Manuel Azaña, himself a keen student of military history. His strategic objective was an army that was financially sound, politically neutral and streamlined for war. But were Azaña's reforms an assault on inefficiency and inertia as he stated, or an attack on the fatherland and its keystone, the army itself?

In June 1931 Azaña closed the 'reactionary' Zaragoza Military Academy and in September of the same year deprived the army of much of its judicial role as the Supreme Military Council was dissolved and the captains-general abolished. Many right-wingers were moved to less important posts or sacked. The army remained under-equipped, notably the artillery.[1] In January 1933 the widely dreaded 'review of promotions' investigated those officers whose careers had been blessed by the Rivera dictatorship (1923–30). Although far fewer were affected than was feared, the myth of a persecuted army was reinforced.

Reassuringly for the army, the Radical leader Lerroux came to power in November 1933 at the head of an increasingly rightist government. Those involved in General Sanjurjo's bungled coup attempt (August 1932) were pardoned. General Franco was promoted to Major General with a special brief to lend expertise on military exercises – a dress-rehearsal for suppressing future left-wing rebellions: when the Asturias Rising broke out in October 1934 it was the Spanish Foreign Legion and Moorish troops whom Franco used on the mainland to such ruthless effect – for the first but not for the last time.[2]

As a reward for his role at Asturias, Franco was made Commander-in-Chief of Spanish Armed Forces in Morocco (his *alma mater*) and, when Gil Robles became Minister of War in May 1935, he became Chief of the General Staff. Other generals such as Fanjul and Goded were plotting a coup should the left be returned to power, but the increasingly influential and prestigious Franco had sound professional reasons for not becoming involved.

Nevertheless, by the time the 'Popular Front' came to power in February 1936, preparations for a military uprising had begun. The new government seemed obsessively biased against the right: Prime Minister Azaña pardoned those workers and left-wing soldiers involved in the Asturias and other risings; the reform programme of 1931–3 was revived; and Franco and Mola were redeployed, with the aim of neutralizing their potential as plotters: Franco to the Canary Islands and Mola to Pamplona in Navarre (conveniently far from Madrid; but, for Mola, conveniently close to Carlist conspirators).

At the rural grass roots in this spring of 1936 peasants were seizing land *en masse*. Right-wing newspapers were promoting an atmosphere of impending doom, encouraging the army right in its plots, the conservative classes praying for their success. With the abandonment in April of one such plot by an ailing general, Rodriguez del Barrio, it was General Mola who was designated coordinator of a future army rising. The month of May began with massed parades by the left and a general strike invoked by the anarchist CNT. Very soon now Mola would reveal to his co-conspirators his master-plan – part centripetal (starting in the provinces), part centrifugal (emanating from Madrid). The growth of Aragonese and Castilian separatism in June 1936 intensified the pressure for a pre-emptive *putsch*.[3] But, as has been seen, Prime Minister Casares Quiroga seemed blind to rumours that such a threat was looming.

The murder of the leading 'catastrophist' right-winger Calvo Sotelo on 13 July finally wedded Franco to the rebellion. On 19 July Franco arrived in Morocco, and by the next day most of the mainland garrisons had risen. However, they only achieved partial success. About 70 per cent of Spain remained beyond their grasp, including the main industrial areas, notably in the Basque Country and Catalonia.

ANALYSIS (1): WHY, AND TO WHAT EXTENT, DID THE ARMY OPPOSE THE SECOND REPUBLIC?

The Spanish army's deep resentment of politicians went back many decades, not least to the imperial disasters of 1898. So did the army's intervention in high politics – and its suppression of grassroots left-wing revolts. However, the history of the Rivera dictatorship and its short-lived successors, as well as that of the Second Republic, showed that many in the armed forces were themselves left-wing, for example, Ramón Franco, anarchist aviator brother of the future Chief of State. Francisco Franco himself was ambivalent about the peacetime Republic (April 1931–July 1936). On the one hand, he derided Republican officers promoted during the 'two reformist years' (1931–3); on the other, he had reason to be grateful for the 'bienio negro' (black biennium) which followed.[4] Indeed, Franco was to play a significant auxiliary role in government during that time. At the outset, it had been two leading generals, Sanjurjo (the Director General of the Civil Guard) and Berenguer (Minister of War) who had in April 1931 made the Republic possible by not standing by the King and not obstructing the popular will.

However, from the first weeks of the Republic military plots to overthrow it were being hatched. Military hostility to the Republic reflected both public and private concerns. 'Publicly', the early Republican governments had displaced the monarchy, attacked the Church and landownership, and threatened to degrade the wholeness of Spain with their policy of autonomy for Catalonia. The constitution declared the Republic to be a 'Republic of *workers*', which alienated the conservatives. Furthermore, communism, much less subversively influential than Franco thought, became the future Caudillo's *bête rouge* as he consumed vast quantities of anti-Comintern propaganda. But what made the 'red threat' only too real was the revolution that was occurring in the Civil War Republican zone from July 1936, a factor that inevitably strengthened the Nationalists' *casus belli*. Freemasonry, a secret order which cut across national loyalties, was another scapegoat for the army right's resentment, while Hugh Thomas makes the interesting additional point that Sanjurjo, Mola and Franco saw the Spanish mainland as a Morocco writ large, 'infested by rebellious tribes masquerading as political parties'.[5]

Gil Robles had seen governments with himself as Prime Minister as *ipso facto* in the national interest, but he was *not* made Premier, in 1933, or in May or December 1935, much to the chagrin of the army right. Even worse, another right-wing politician with a messianic claim to lead, José Calvo Sotelo, was murdered in the cataclysmic month of July 1936 by a hit-squad led by a Communist captain of the Civil Guard.

On the 'personal' level of issues more directly affecting the army, Michael Alpert offers in his essay *Soldiers, Politics and War* (1984) revealing insights into the long-standing sensitivity of the army to criticism.[6] In the first years of the Second Republic itself, the army had to contend with Azaña's military reforms, the earliest of which were promulgated by decree rather than by a parliament, thus placing their legitimacy in doubt. Personal grudges abounded. Sanjurjo was demoted in early 1932 and, after the *Sanjurjada* coup attempt, was sent to a grim civilian jail. Franco was dismissed as Commandant of the Zaragoza Military Academy, which, adding national insult to personal injury, was closed down by the despised Azaña. In 1933, in what he saw as professional banishment, Franco was sent to become General Officer Commanding, Balearic Islands, and in 1936 was catapulted 'out of mischief' to the Canaries. Goded, too, had personal reasons for regarding the Republic with contempt, though his feelings were less cannily disguised than Franco's. But resentment was not exclusive to the army right – naturally enough, its keenly Republican wing condemned favours to rightists granted by the Lerroux–Gil Robles governments.

These 'public' and 'personal' factors combine to give some idea of why the rising in July 1936 was seen as 'necessary'. Moreover, the *alzamiento*, as it was called, was not only a reaction to the total catastrophe into which the *Patria* appeared to have been plunged but, according to Carr, was timed to outflank the arrival at barracks of the new, Republican draft.[7]

What, then, made the rising possible? Paul Preston makes the telling point that those officers who took retirement in 1931 now had time on their hands to plot.[8] Individually, this may have had little significance, but by the summer of 1936 a broad coalition of army and civilian interests existed. Mola had established links to Alfonsists, to Carlists, to Franco, to the UME and to the Madrid Police HQ. Gil Robles was providing money; Italian and German arms had been sought by Generals Barrera and Franco respectively. The Spanish army's own military capability had been enhanced by both Azaña and Gil Robles as Ministers of War; and if in a perverse sense this was an error of judgement, others are less debatable, such as moving Mola to Pamplona in early 1936 – a damage-limitation exercise that backfired. Thus the master-plan was coalescing well and by mid-July Franco too was on board. Fundamentally, the army, despite assaults upon it, still had power, as had the German Reichswehr after the Versailles *Diktat*.

The realities of experience for the army (as army, and as citizens with a responsibility to uphold the honour of the *Patria*) are inescapable: sweeping reform, left-wing agitation and amnesties for the left, whether Jaca mutineers (November 1932) or the Asturistas of October 1934. However, the army's bitterness also derived from threats (to make retirement compulsory), fears (would Azaña replace the army with a red militia?) and assumptions (that Azaña was bewitched by a 'black cabinet' of Republican officers).

Turning now to the second part of this analysis, namely the extent to which the army opposed the Second Republic, various sources have offered quantitative assessments. Preston, for example, has calculated that from the very beginning of the Second Republic a considerable number of officers were unequivocally republican but that a larger group had grave doubts about the new political system; nevertheless, that in July 1936 only four out of twenty-one major (i.e. full) generals supported the *alzamiento*. Thomas's estimate for 1931 is that about half of the officer corps were 'apolitical opportunists', with various minorities either radical, republican or right-wing. Hills's research suggested that only 10 per cent of officers supported the notion of a rebellion.[9] But what seems inescapable is that from early 1936 there would be a significant, though not overwhelming, increase in the number of conspirators.

What of Francisco Franco, whose image as a ruthless belligerent has clouded the reality of the positions he adopted towards the Republic? It could easily be assumed that Franco opposed it. In fact, despite Azaña's reforms, he was grudgingly tolerant, by necessity if not by choice. He may never have supported the Republic as an ideal, but he was prepared to engage with specific governments who were 'restoring honour, discipline, the basics'[10] and whose priorities were the defence of the social order and the Catholic faith. Moreover, under the Lerroux–Robles governments Franco and other rightists were promoted, and the red cloud of Asturias was evaporated by the brutal heat of their repression. Franco much admired Gil Robles's reforms as Minister of War; and when ministers lacked detailed knowledge of things military, they turned to Franco for advice. Even so, when the durability of rightist governments was in doubt – for example, Lerroux's in September 1933 – Franco was wary and would not accept office. More consistently, he distanced himself from plans for a military coup until February 1936 when, following the PF victory, he sounded out the solidity of his colleagues' opinions for or against an insurrection.

Others, in the earlier years of the Republic, were less circumspect. For those such as General Orgaz, to conspire was their *raison d'être*. However, it might be taken for granted that Africanistas, Army of Africa veterans, necessarily opposed the Republic. But the Africanista General Pozas, Director General of the Civil Guard after Sanjurjo, was a loyal Republican who refused to respond to Franco's probings in February 1936. Equally loyal was Francisco Franco's cousin, the Republican leader in Tetuan, Morocco, whose execution in 1936 Francisco chillingly endorsed. Others came to oppose the Republic over a period of time: for example, General Queipo de Llano, son-in-law of the President but merciless chief of the Seville rising in July 1936. For Francisco Franco himself, support for the Republic was always qualified, but a number of further personal slights, notably removal as Chief of the General Staff by Quiroga in early 1936, corroded his already problematical 'loyalty'. General Mola, mastermind of the July 1936 *alzamiento*, only began to plot seriously during that year, whereas Generals Sanjurjo and Goded were committed conspirators much earlier. It was Goded who in August 1932 launched the abortive *Sanjurjada* in Madrid. Though feeble in execution, as with Hitler's Munich Putsch nine years before, the thinking behind the *Sanjurjada* did not lack passion. Had not the Second Republic set anarchy loose on the beloved *Patria*? Why did it not defend its own security forces? How could it be allowed to abuse sacred tradition? But the organization and the support were lacking. On the other hand, when General Rodriguez del Barrio plotted in the spring of 1936 he had more support, but various factors, including his own terminal illness, conspired to render his putsch stillborn.

Formal regimental organization alone would have held back the growth of a convincing conspiratorial base. Thus an underground movement, the Spanish Military Union (UME), was set up in 1933 to liaise secretly between garrisons. By 1935 it could claim members in all eight military regions and links with CEDA, the Alfonsists and the Carlists. Generals Goded and Fanjul were members. Franco, though he kept abreast of its activities, was not. Many other generals were sceptical, too, and Hills is very critical of UME's performance in July 1936.[11] The pro-Republican challenge took the form of the Republican Antifascist Military Union (UMRA). Founded in 1934 by left-wing officers to oppose the UME and uphold the original ideals of the Republic, the UMRA was significant at various levels. It helped forge the PSOE (Socialist) militia into a serious fighting unit, while Stanley G. Payne has suggested that the UMRA was manipulated by the Communist Party (PCE) through a Marxist on the General Staff.[12] Some police officers were UMRA; so was José Castillo, the Assault Guard lieutenant whose murder led to the (unpunished) assassination of José Calvo Sotelo on 13 July 1936.

Without military opponents, and supporters, of the Republic there would have been no Civil War. By letters, speeches, almost-candidacies (at one point Franco might have become a CEDA Deputy), organizations and conspiracies, the army right expressed anti-republican emotions ranging from extreme scepticism to downright loathing. Even so, the Second Republic experienced five years and three months of 'peace'. From July 1936, though, the latent became manifest: two years and nine months of war were to test the Republic's powers beyond endurance.

Questions

1. How representative was Francisco Franco of military opinion during the Second Republic?
2. How far can it be said that a military rising was 'inevitable' after February 1936?

ANALYSIS (2): WHY, DURING THE PERIOD APRIL 1931 TO DECEMBER 1935, DID THE ARMY NOT STAGE A LARGE-SCALE REVOLT?

There was, during these years, plenty to provoke collective anxiety and revulsion within army circles, not just in the realm of military matters *per se*. But of widespread, carefully coordinated physical revolt there was no evidence. The one attempted military coup, the *Sanjurjada* of August 1932, was carried out by a tiny minority; Azaña's government countered the rebels with ease, sentenced Sanjurjo to death, commuted to 'life', and purged several hundred officers. Such was warning enough to those prone to active dissent.

Moreover, the army, most of whom had sworn an oath of loyalty to the Republic, was institutionalized within the new system, both in government itself and its police affiliates, the rural Civil Guard and urban Assault Guard, both led by soldiers and composed largely of ex-army personnel. Furthermore, in 1931–3 Republican officers such as General Masquelet were given top positions, while NCOs gained special status at army college. Conversely, from November 1933 to February 1936 the army right helped see to it that the values and priorities of 'traditional' Spain were once again given due respect.

The implication, then, is that the army was divided in itself during this period and thus incapable of a large-scale revolt. Admittedly, these divisions predated the Republic; but many were aware of what Franco called the army's lack of 'moral unity' after April 1931. Franco was also bitterly critical of impetuous hotheads who assumed that they could launch a restoration of some supposed past glory by virtue of their zeal alone. Indeed, there were many besides Franco who can better be described as 'accidentalists' rather than 'catastrophists', believing that much could be achieved within the framework of the Republic, not least massive retaliation against 'communism'. The policies and achievements of right-wing governments from November 1933 suggested that a coup was unnecessary: for example, the Ministry of the Interior dealt harshly with the trade union movement, and the October 1934 risings were defeated. The left was thus weakened while the Church and landowning classes were strengthened. CEDA was not prevented from entering government; Franco and others were given plum postings and were impressed when Minister of War Gil Robles not only reopened the Zaragoza Military Academy but motorized some army units and raised ammunition production.[13]

It had, however, been apparent that the liberal reforms of 1931–3 associated with the Alcalá Zamora and Azaña governments, which hardly amounted to 'red revolution', were popular with many Spaniards. Nor had public opinion become sufficiently polarized to justify, in the interests of Spain 'saving itself from itself', a large-scale revolt. The bizarre *Sanjurjada* had buttressed public opinion in favour of the government. Meanwhile, Azaña's military reforms did not, and did not seek to, castrate the army: its judicial powers were not completely rescinded and there was no blind purge of the officer corps.[14] Indeed, Azaña was capable of even-handed policies, notably on promotions procedures, designed to reconcile opposing military factions to the regime.

Whatever the case, the failed coup attempts during the Rivera dictatorship (1923–30), whether by army right or army left, were all too vivid in the army's memory, and it seemed unrealistic to put the clock back to an Alfonsine monarchy, 'military' or otherwise. Even if a minority sought such a reversion, theirs was but one viewpoint on a broad horizon of dissent.

The phenomenon of the Civil Guard poses something of a problem for this analysis. Why was it thought they could not be relied upon (witness their absence from the *Sanjurjada*, which reinforced Franco's resistance to putschism)? After all, they had a brutal reputation in their dealings with the left and, logically, should have welcomed overtures to establish a rigid and permanent authoritarian system of the right. However, the Civil Guard was an arm of the state, not of insurrection. It saw its role as the defence of social order, though it is true that when government was seen to be undermining that order, for example, via land reform, then the Civil Guard remained loyal to the landowners. For the latter, the Civil Guard was reliability personified: it helped to break strikes and pressurize electors to vote for their 'masters'. Not least because the

Civil Guard got as good as it gave against the left, it could be merciless: at Arnedo in 1932, at Casas Viejas in 1933 and at Asturias in 1934. But whether it would risk its own position and that of its principal mentor, the state, by backing rickety attempts by the army to seize power was another matter altogether.

Some in the Civil Guard were themselves left-wing, as the murder of Calvo Sotelo in July 1936 was to demonstrate. The first Republican governments, however, were clearly aware of the Civil Guard's traditionally anti-liberal credentials and in October 1931 established the Assault Guards as a modern police force exclusive to, and fully supportive of, the Republic. After the *Sanjurjada* the 'Asaltos' were doubled to 10,000. They were again increased after the October 1934 Asturias Rising. Ultimately, therefore, a different question from 'Could the Civil Guard be relied upon to support a military coup?' might be asked, namely, 'Was a military coup necessary if the Civil and Assault Guards were doing such a rigorous job repressing the far left?'

In conclusion, the preconditions for a large-scale military revolt did not exist until well after December 1935. There were both internal and external obstructions that prevented any movement from becoming a sustained insurrection. The chain of command within the militant army right was yet to be developed. A 'catastrophist' consensus was still to emerge. Italy and Germany had promised help, but not enough to guarantee success. Gil Robles had not yet transferred CEDA money to the insurrectionist cause; Calvo Sotelo, as much a potential ally as a rival, had spent much of the period in exile. Franco did not trust the Falange (though he was later to use them) and the UME lacked a cutting edge. Most in the Civil and Assault Guards could not be prised from the state. Not in August 1932 (the *Sanjurjada*), or in October 1934 (after the Asturias and other risings), or in December 1935 (moves to make Gil Robles Prime Minister with army backing) was there sufficient support for military coercion against the Republic. The pivotal figure of Francisco Franco remained unattached, if not disinterested. Ultimately, however, military opposition to the Republic between April 1931 and December 1935 took the form not so much of coup attempts as threats, think-tanks and clandestine cells. The language spoken may have been that of insurrection, but neither rhetoric nor aspiration could be translated into large-scale revolt, let alone victory.

Questions

1. What advantages did the Republic possess in its relations with the Spanish Army?

2. What was the significance of General Sanjurjo's coup attempt in August 1932?

SOURCES

1. MOTIVES OF FRANCO AND HIS NATIONALIST SUPPORTERS

Source A: from Franco's *Manifesto de las Palmas*, 17 July 1936.

Nothing has checked the lust for power; the illegal dismissal of moderating elements; glorification of the Asturian and Catalan revolutions, the one and the other violating the Constitution . . .

Can we consent one day longer to the shameful spectacle we are presenting to the world? . . .

Justice and Equality before the law we offer you; peace and love between Spaniards. Liberty and Fraternity without libertinage and tyranny. Work for all. Social justice, accomplished without rancour or violence, and an equitable and progressive distribution of wealth without destroying or jeopardizing the Spanish economy.

But face to face with this, a war without quarter on the exploiters of politics, on the deceivers of the honest worker, on the foreigners and foreign-oriented people who openly or deceitfully endeavour to destroy Spain . . .

Our impulse is not determined by the defence of some bastard interests; nor by the desire to retrace our steps in the road of history.

Source B: from *Joint Letter of the Spanish Bishops to the Bishops of the Whole World Concerning the War in Spain*, 1 July 1937.

Coinciding in the same initial moment of the conflict the [civic-military Movement and the Communist revolution] mark, from the beginning of the war, the deep division of the two Spains which were to contend on the battlefields . . . The War is therefore like an armed plebiscite . . .

But, above all, the Revolution was anti-Christian. We do not believe that in the history of Christianity and in the interval of a few weeks there has occurred such an explosion of hatred, in all forms of thought, will, and passion, against Jesus Christ and His sacred religion. So great have been the sacrilegious ravages suffered by the Church in Spain that the delegate of the Spanish Reds sent to the Congress of the Godless in Moscow was able to say: 'Spain has surpassed in a great degree the work of the Soviets, as the Church in Spain has been completely annihilated.'

Source C: Harold Cardozo's pro-Franco perspective, 1937.

It became obvious that things were going from bad to worse, and that a complete upheaval could not be long delayed. The Azaña hangers-on were afraid to accept the help of the Army for fear they should be obliged to abandon part of their political campaigns of greed and anti-religious hatred, while, on the other hand, they submitted to the almost open blackmail of the Red extremists . . .

But . . . these Army officers, trained to respect discipline, law and order, imbued with the traditions of Christian Spain . . . felt in the great majority that they could not accept the imposition, by a minority, of the atheistic principles of Moscow on Spain. They decided that if things did not improve, the Army would have to do once more what it had so often done in the past, take over the government of the country itself . . .

The Army movement . . . was the justifiable defence of the 'real Spain' against deadly menace from abroad. It had the support, not only of the two strong political parties, the Carlists and the Falangists, but of the great mass of the people – workers, middle class, and aristocrats alike.

Source D: writing in exile, ex-Foreign Minister Julio Alvarez del Vayo defends the Republic.

With the exception of this spontaneous and natural mobilization of the masses to demand an amnesty, nothing happened until the month of July to justify the accusations of anarchy and chaos levelled against the Government, by the Fascist conspirators the better to cloak their own subversive activities. What did happen was, in fact, largely a concomitant of the preparations for the rebellion which were going on actively from the week following the elections. *Agents provocateurs* abounded . . . Moreover, there was complicity on the part of many men in Governmental agencies, civil governors, Civil Guard commanders, and others who, charged with the sacred duty of keeping order, connived at provoking disorder . . . But the violence of these months has been greatly exaggerated and repeatedly men like Gil Robles and Calvo Sotelo, engaged in actively preparing the rebellion, stood up in Parliament and read inflated lists of church burnings and other supposed outbreaks as a part of their revolutionary propaganda . . .

Neither could the Right-wing extremists at that time bring any allegations of diabolic influence against the Soviet Embassy, for there was no Soviet ambassador in Spain, nor had there ever been one since the Russian Revolution.

Source E: Poem on the Antiquity of Spain (A Russian Tank in Castile) by the Falangist poet Agustín de Foxá, published 1940.

Russian tanks, Siberian snows,
In these noble Spanish fields,
What hope has the poppy against your cold bulk?
What can the poplar by the river oppose to your fury?

We still had oxen and wooden ploughs.
Castile is not scientific; no factories are
Raised on her soil; her clay produces, like Athens,
Theogonies and olive trees, battles, kings and gods . . .
To win Spain, you have to say, like Christ:
'My kingdom is not of this world'; don't raise sickles
Or promise the body earthly paradises,
For in Spain voices surge forth from the sepulchres.
Because there are genealogy, race and prayers,
Because the child who is born is already 2,000 years old
And, with the demeanour of kings, his shepherds rule.
Come, Russian chariots, ugly machines,
Animals without blood, mate or sweat.

With a little fire, just as someone burns a tree,
In your heavy tracks you'll be brought to a halt.
And the earth will cover you and the rain and the ants,
The lark of the skies and the flowers of the fields.
And as your rust returns to the land
Castile will again fill her horizon with Saints.

Questions

1. Define (i) 'Congress of the Godless' (Source B); (ii) 'agents provocateurs' (Source D). (2)
2. Considering the language and tone of Source A, how does Franco seek to persuade Spaniards that the Nationalist cause is *their* cause? (5)
3. How reliable do you consider Source C as an assessment of political allegiances in Spain in 1936? (4)
*4. Discuss the ways in which the author of Source E contrasts Spanish tradition and *Hispanidad* with the 'alien' presence of Russia and Marxism. (6)
5. Making use of the sources and your own knowledge, how important, and how convincing, was the 'threat of communism' in explaining support for the Nationalist cause? (7)

Worked answer

4. [A good way to begin this question would be to list Spanish and Russian references in two columns in order to develop a range of contrasting images.]

In this poem, Foxá contrasts Castilian tradition with Russian imperialism by juxtaposing communist imagery and ideas ('sickles', as in hammer and sickle; 'earthly [i.e. materialistic] paradises') against symbols of eternal, united Spain, of which Castile is held to be the crucible. Indigenous natural phenomena (blood-red poppies, tall and dignified poplars) are contrasted with the cold and sterile form of Russian tanks, 'animals without blood, mate or sweat'. And a powerful thread of religious imagery underlines how the spiritual essence of Spanish nationhood can never assimilate the finite, inorganic and perishable values of communism. Foxá brings out this theme of unassailable tradition and potent spirituality by reference to 'theogonies', the classical Athenian world of divine heroes. He also makes use of Christian references, ending five consecutive lines with: 'sepulchres . . . heavens . . . prayers . . . two thousand years old . . . his shepherds rule'. Furthermore, romantic references to Spain's rural traditions ('noble Spanish fields'; 'oxen and wooden ploughs') are set against 'this' world of alien factories. Projecting this contrast into the future, Foxá suggests that whereas the fertile Spanish race will give birth to devout generations as yet beyond the horizon, the invader will be consumed by the Spanish earth. The ironic references to 'what hope?' and 'what can?' (lines 3 and 4) further underline the author's confidence in Spain's destiny. Spain, with Castile as its spiritual core, is seen in this poem as a beacon of faith, an enduring culture, against which communist iconoclasm is doomed to fail.

SOURCES

2. GERMAN AND ITALIAN AID TO THE INSURGENTS TO MARCH 1937

Source F: journalist Goronwy Rees on reasons for intervention, August 1936.

In ordinary times the civil war might have raged in isolation behind the Pyrenees, as in some African province of Europe, but in the troubled circumstances of today it threatens to divide Europe . . . and cause a war of intervention . . .

It is not difficult to find motives for intervention . . . A rebel victory resulting in a Fascist pro-Italian Spain would threaten Gibraltar and the route to India: and General Franco is reported to be willing, in return for Italian help, to cede Ceuta and the Balearic Isles to Signor Mussolini and make the Mediterranean an Italian lake. Further, a Fascist Spain would be yet another enemy on the French frontier, and, with Italy, a means of cutting her communications with French Morocco. These military and naval advantages would mean an immense accession of strength to the Fascist countries. But the civil war also invites intervention on grounds of political and intellectual sympathy. The revolt has so far intensified the political struggle in Spain that the defeat of the rebels would, in all probability, be followed . . . by an administration of the extreme Left . . . General Franco has presented Europe with the choice between a Fascist or a Communist Spain.

Source G: Ribbentrop recalls Hitler's fears in 1936.

Germany could not tolerate a Communist Spain under any circumstances. As a National Socialist [Hitler] had the obligation to do everything to prevent that eventuality . . . If a Communist Spain actually does emerge, in view of the current situation in France the Bolshevisation of that country is only a matter of a short time and then Germany can 'pack up' [*einpacken*]. Hemmed in between the powerful Soviet bloc in the East and a strong Franco-Spanish communist bloc in the West we could hardly do anything, if Moscow decides to act against Germany.

Source H: a German government communiqué, 18 November 1936.

Since the Government of General Franco has taken possession of the greater part of the Spanish national territory and since developments of the past weeks have shown . . . that no responsible government authority can be said to exist any longer in the rest of Spain, the German Government has decided to recognise the Government of General Franco and to appoint a chargé d'affair[e]s to it for the purpose of taking up diplomatic relations.

Source I: the Italian Minister Plenipotentiary in Tangier to Count Ciano (Italian Foreign Minister), 19 August 1936.

Speedy Italian commitment to ample assistance then permitted Franco to turn around his difficult predicament and gave him the freedom of movement to become master of Western Spain and occupy the Sierra de Guadarrama before the capital. But, from such positions, solid and important that they are, he can only with difficulty go forward and secure above all possession of the capital if he does not have new resources to make up the deficiencies in his armament and to balance the help constantly sent by the forces of international subversion, especially the French Popular Front.

Source J: Arthur Koestler, writing in 1937.

The military insurrection broke out on July 18, 1936.

Two weeks later the rebels were in possession of a brand-new air-fleet of German and Italian planes, manned by German and Italian pilots, mechanics and instructors; Italian tanks were already in action at Badajoz; Irun was being bombarded by German heavy artillery . . . Technicians also were pouring into the country . . . Italian regular troops landed in Majorca; and by the end of October this largest of the Balearic Islands had become virtually an Italian possession. Week by week the number of foreigners in the rebel army grew.

On November 18, by which time the capital and three fifths of Spain were in the hands of the constitutionally elected Government, Germany and Italy proclaimed General Franco ruler of Spain.

During the winter months of 1936–7, Italy landed 85–90,000 infantry in Spain, while Germany took over various specialised technical functions in the rebel army: motor transport, tanks and anti-tank guns, anti-aircraft guns, coastal batteries, and heavy artillery.

On February 9, 1937, the Italians captured Malaga . . .

The Spanish War is for the dictatorships in many respects a dress rehearsal for the world war for which it is preparing the way.

Questions

1. For the Nationalists, what was the significance of the Republicans' loss of:
   (a) Badajoz;
   (b) Irún? (Source J) (4)
2. How does Source G make more explicit German anxieties suggested in the latter part of Source F? (3)
3. How convincing an assessment of the situation in Spain is provided by Source H? (4)
*4. Study Source J. In what seems to be a largely factual account of Italian and German intervention, how might the reader detect an underlying purpose on the part of the writer? (5)
5. How adequate are these sources in explaining the motivation and impact of Italian and German intervention in Spain up to March 1937? (9)

Worked answer

*4. [Look closely at language and tone, and use any knowledge you may have of Koestler's personal experience of the Spanish Civil War.]

Without further knowledge of the context, and on first reading, Source J could indeed be seen as a mere inventory of Fascist and Nazi aid to Franco. Closer scrutiny, however, reveals more. In effect, Koestler's prose reaches beyond surgical dissection of that aid and acquires the force of a politically and morally driven exposé. His language and tone imply that the dictators' assault on the 'constitutionally elected' government is not only illegitimate but imperialistic. Thus Franco is 'proclaimed' (not 'recognized') as ruler of Spain, as if the Caudillo were a puppet; the Italians 'capture' Malaga and preside in Majorca, and Germans 'take over' specialized technical functions. At all cardinal points of the compass, this is an aid programme in overdrive, 'pouring in', 'week by week'. And it is massive aid in breadth. Not only do Hitler and Mussolini upgrade Franco's war machine with state-of-the-art weapons of attack and defence; they provide the personnel to ensure that the weapons are lethal. Ominously, Koestler infers an ulterior motive beyond victory for Franco – namely, effective preparation for a wider conflict yet to come. Koestler, who was himself arrested by the Nationalists in February 1937, had been covering the Spanish Civil War for the *News Chronicle*, an English newspaper demanding British government intervention for the Republic. Koestler's own politics were communist: he had joined the KPD two years before Hitler became Chancellor of Germany, and he was a propaganda writer for the Comintern. Therefore, Koestler would be driven to do more than list, clinically, Hitler's and Mussolini's aid to Franco's rebel forces. His underlying message is that, in order to crush fascism, the balance of foreign aid must be resolutely redressed.[15]

4

THE REPUBLIC'S RESPONSE

BACKGROUND NARRATIVE

The twelve turbulent months from mid-July 1936 showed significant, though not decisive, advances against the Republic by the rebel forces of Mola and Franco. These victories followed their initial failure to seize power in a coordinated coup throughout Spain. They had been successful in areas that centred on Pamplona in Navarre, Vitoria in the neighbouring Basque province of Alava, Zaragoza in Aragón, Burgos in Old Castile, Valladolid in León and La Coruña in Galicia. In the south of Spain, in Andalucía, their prizes, again often after fierce initial resistance, included Seville, Granada, Cádiz and Córdoba. The rebel insurgents, or Nationalists (Nacionales) also controlled Morocco, the Canaries and the Balearic Islands (except for Minorca). Their forces now proceeded to take Badajoz (Estremadura) in August, and Toledo (New Castile) and San Sebastián (in the agriculture- and industry-rich Basque province of Guipúzcoa) in September. In October the Republican siege of Oviedo, capital of Asturias, was lifted.

The capture of Badajoz and Toledo from the Republic had marked important steps in the Nationalist advance from the south-west on Madrid, the outskirts of which were reached in early November 1936. Attempts to take the city by frontal assault were abandoned by 23 November, and in December General Franco changed to a strategy of encirclement. But neither the Battle of the Jarama (February 1937) nor the Battle of Guadalajara in March achieved this goal. The

Nationalists' focus now switched once more to the northern front: at the end of March General Mola opened a new offensive in the Basque province of Vizcaya. The devastating fire-bombing of Guernica took place in April and by mid-June 1937 the port and industrial city of Bilbao had fallen to the Nationalists. But two weeks later on 6 July it was to be the Republican Popular Army that took the offensive: at Brunete on the Madrid front it attempted to relieve pressure on the north and to split the Nationalists west of the capital. However, this Republican success was to be short-lived. Furthermore, by this time the USSR had significantly changed its strategy from assisting in the Republic's victory to helping to delay its defeat. Recruitment into the Comintern-organized International Brigades began to fall.

Twelve months before, the Republic had had no international aid at all – in contrast to the Nationalists whose assistance from Nazi Germany and Fascist Italy had kept their rebellion afloat after its failure to achieve outright victory. On 18–19 July 1936, with military revolt against 'communism, separatism and anarchy' biting into the Republic, the governments of Casares Quiroga and Martínez Barrio fell in rapid succession. The new Prime Minister, Giral, at last armed the Communist militia (MAOC), Socialist trade union (UGT) and anarchist CNT, previously denied weapons for fear they would be used for revolution. More anti-fascist militias were formed, for example, in Barcelona where the military rebels had also failed to seize power. By early September Giral had been replaced as Prime Minister by Largo Caballero. Largo headed a Popular Front government led by Socialists, Communists and Left Republicans. At the end of that month a more efficient Popular Army was created out of the militias. Though Britain, France and the United States adopted an official policy of non-intervention, the first Russian military aid to the Republic arrived in mid-October 1936, and the Popular Army was reorganized into brigades. On 7 November, with the Largo Caballero government relocating to Valencia on the eastern coast, the protection of Madrid fell to a 'Defence Junta' under General Miaja. Now the International Brigades began to join the Republican forces in strength, playing a vital role in the military defence of the capital along with the predominantly Communist 'Fifth Regiment' under Colonel Enrique Líster. Nationalist attempts in February and March 1937 to encircle the capital were repulsed.

Besides these military confrontations, the period from July 1936 witnessed both Republican and Nationalist terror campaigns in their respective zones. Hundreds of thousands of civilians were murdered. Within the Republican zone a social and economic revolution of sorts established collectives in both agriculture and industry, though these transformations were controversial: would they really help to win the war? Political disputes undermined Republican unity, not least in Catalonia where in March 1937 the anarchist CNT quit the regional government, the Generalitat. By early May the CNT and anti-Stalinist POUM were literally at war with the Catalan government and Communist Party. On 15 May Largo Caballero resigned as Prime Minister, to be replaced by fellow-Socialist Juan Negrín, and his ringing mandate: 'Victory at all costs'.

ANALYSIS (1): WHY DID THE MILITARY RISING NOT ACHIEVE IMMEDIATE CONTROL OF SPAIN?

Was the failure due to its inability to capture key centres such as Madrid, Bilbao and Santander in the north, Barcelona and Valencia in the east, Badajoz in the west, and Málaga and Jaén in the south? Indeed, a coordinated enveloping attack on the capital in July 1936 proved impossible. Forty years later, in *The Battle for Madrid*, the Anglo-Spanish writer and broadcaster George Hills made this point explicit: for example, that because of fighting on the northern Basque and Santander fronts, the rebels could only commit part of VI Divisional Command's forces to a march south on the capital; and their advance was blocked eighty kilometres short, at the passes through the Guadarrama Mountains.[1]

In Madrid itself, the leadership of the poorly coordinated and undermanned coup attempt had fallen to the second-in-command, General Fanjul. But Fanjul found himself besieged in the Montaña Barracks ('a hated symbol of reaction and military repression')[2] and outnumbered two to one by well-trained Assault and Civil Guards and by the MAOC (Communist) and UGT (Socialist) militias. The revolt also collapsed at other barracks in Madrid, but it was the Montaña – source of the 50,000 bolts missing from rifles distributed by the government – that provided the crucial victory. Many loyalists now marched to lay siege to the Alcázar in Toledo, to which in turn Franco would divert his forces, giving Madrid yet more breathing space.

Historians also underline the importance of the Assault and Civil Guards in putting down the rebellion in Barcelona – Spain's largest port and second-most populous city. However, writers such as Jackson, Mitchell, Esenwein and Shubert, and Preston stress the initiatives taken by the anarchist CNT and independent Marxist POUM militias in seizing arms and defeating what was in any case a half-hearted revolt. Sources quoted in Fraser's innovative oral history, *Blood of Spain*, point to a mutual dependency between civilian resistance and security forces loyal to the Republic. But whatever the case, the loyal Assault and Civil Guards in Barcelona outnumbered the insurgents; and the workers seized arms the government had refused to distribute. Rebel general Goded, who had flown into this humiliating situation from Majorca, lacked the military power base for a successful coup. But his defeat had a much wider significance for, as Paul Preston has observed, with Barcelona secure for the Republic, so was Catalonia. Catalonia's resources would do much to sustain the Republican war effort. The Catalan historian Albert Balcells underlines the weakness of Carlism and the Falange in Catalonia, and the opposition to the coup by the Catalan Regional League (Lliga). Therefore, the 'political constituency' in Catalonia was deeply unsympathetic to the military revolt. Even where the rebels were in the narrower sense locally successful, the wider environment might well remain hostile to them, as in Galicia, Andalucía, and the coal-rich Asturias with its explosives industry.

Thus, in terms of resources, the Republic retained several advantages in July 1936. Besides Catalonia and Asturias (minus its capital, Oviedo), these included the industry of the Basque provinces and the fruit- and vegetable-rich Mediterranean lands. The Republican zone's population was double that of the rebels'; it had 75 per cent of railway engines and rolling stock, Spain's gold reserves and its main radio stations. This last point is crucial, for the government's report that the uprising in Morocco had been put down led to hesitation on the mainland, and to the revolt's collapse in Valencia and elsewhere. The radio was also used significantly in Barcelona, where President Companys persuaded General Goded to broadcast the surrender call to his troops. In Bilbao telephone taps prevented a revolt from ever getting off the ground.

What was the balance of Republican loyalism and rebel insurgency among the armed forces themselves? In their 1936 account for the Left Book Club, *Spain in Revolt*, Gannes and Repard noted that the Spanish air force was a relatively new phenomenon, its officers mainly middle class; here, 'remnants of feudalism' had failed to gain much of a foothold. But the percentage of air force personnel joining the rising has been disputed. Whereas Payne estimated only about 20 per cent pro-rebellion, Hills's (1976) figure is double that.[3]

Whatever indiscipline and ineffective leadership followed the naval mutinies against rebel officers in July 1936, the fact remains that most of the Spanish navy remained loyal to the Republic and consequently the rebels suffered a crucial initial setback: Franco's army was blockaded in Morocco by both surface ships and submarines.

George Hills's estimate of the balance of Spanish army personnel is useful because it is dated 22 July, after the military risings against the Republic had occurred. Also, the estimate excludes the blockaded Army of Africa. Thus, based on Hills's statistics, the Nationalist rebels had: 53 per cent of the army (all ranks); 17 per cent of major (i.e. most senior) generals; but 46 per cent of brigadiers and 65 per cent of junior officers. In addition the rebels only had one intact military region, the VIIth, based on Valladolid in León. Esenwein and Shubert (1995) add the VIth, with its HQ at Burgos in Old Castile. However, this criterion ('intact') is misleading because it excludes other military regions in which the rebels controlled most, or at least a good portion, of the territory. On the matter of rebel officers, Fraser (1979/94) observed that the bulk of those were captains and majors with a lesser number of colonels – but Alpert (1984) observes that most of the younger colonels joined the rebels. Nevertheless, such points of difference aside, the fact remains that the rebel Nationalists lacked sufficient support to achieve what Fraser calls the 'decisive breakthrough' and thus control of Spain in July 1936.[4]

A crucial problem was how to get the Army of Africa from Morocco to the Spanish mainland. Hitherto the rebels had for this purpose only four aircraft at their disposal, so only 130 soldiers per day could be airlifted. Generals Mola and Franco appealed to Germany for help. The German Foreign Ministry opposed intervention: German citizens in Spain and German ships in Spanish waters might be put at risk, as might relations with France and Britain. Indeed, Ribbentrop, German Ambassador to Britain, was working ostensibly for a British alliance. Like Mola, General Franco had cabled the German Foreign Ministry but, similarly rebuffed, cunningly approached the Nazi Party leadership through some German business contacts. Franco's request reached Hitler on 25 July 1936. Having cogitated for two hours, the Führer agreed to help lift the blockade on the Army of Africa – on grounds both strategic (for example, to undermine French security) and ideological (to exorcize the spectre of communism and anarchy). Thus, ten days after the rising had begun in Morocco, on 27 July German Junkers JU52 aircraft began their airlift of Spanish and Moorish troops to the peninsula. Recent scholarship demonstrates that Hitler's decision to help the Nationalists had not been planned in advance.[5]

Italy, too, had originally doubted the wisdom of involvement. On 22 July Mussolini, worried that it might upset Italian diplomacy vis-à-vis France and Britain, declined to assist Franco's colonial forces. Only on 30 July, with the Duce convinced that neither France nor the USSR would intervene in Spain, and with Britain apparently favouring Franco, did Italian planes leave Sardinia for Morocco. This in itself was nearly two weeks after the rising, and the aircraft were not ready to operate as aircover for Franco's convoys until 5 August.

Thus, a painful and to a large extent unforeseen combination of internal and external setbacks robbed the military insurgents of outright victory against the Republic. Writing in 1938, the Duchess of Atholl observed that the rebellion was not in any case a 'popular movement': 'No one has attempted to name any centre in which there was a spontaneous rising of the civil population in their favour.'[6] Perhaps Navarre came nearest to it, with its entrenched anti-Republican Carlism. But to many in Spain the politics of Navarre were as much a furnace of fear as a beacon of hope. Stanley G. Payne wrote in 1970, 'The rebellion that precipitated the revolution and Civil War was not a "generals' revolt" but a rising of the active middle strata of the officer corps that in many cases dragged senior generals along with it.'[7] However, in many cases resistance to the rebels was sustained: a social and economic revolution was launched in the Republican zone, showing a determination to create the polar opposite of what Mola's and Franco's Nationalists represented and respected. And, crucially, Spain's most populous city and its centre of communications, its capital – Madrid – refused to yield to them.

Questions

1. Why could an insurgent victory in July 1936 not be taken for granted?
2. Using maps of the Spanish Civil War, note successive changes to the sizes of the Republican and Nationalist zones and, as your understanding of the Civil War grows, analyse the significance of each.

ANALYSIS (2): WHAT DOES THE DEFENCE OF MADRID REVEAL OF THE STRENGTHS AND WEAKNESSES OF THE REPUBLIC?

By November 1936 a number of positive reforms enabled the Republican side to resist more effectively the Nationalist threat to the national capital. Militiamen and women and regular soldiers had pay rises, and a successful recruitment drive had swelled the ranks of the Assault and Civil (now 'Republican National') Guards. A more robust GOC Central Theatre of Operations had been appointed, and the General Staff reorganized to include commanders of the International Brigades and 'Fifth Regiment'. Militias became regular units of the People's Army and self-sufficient 'mixed brigades' were brought in. All this was varnished by glowing tributes from the Prime Minister, Largo Caballero. Yet his rhetoric was misleading. On 28 October he hailed the 'heroic sons of the worker-people', and called on them to 'hurl fire' against the traitorous enemy: *'Victory is yours!'* Only nine days later, however, he and his cabinet left for the east coast and the 'safe haven' of Valencia.

With Largo's departure, General Miaja and his colleagues in the new Madrid 'Defence Junta' began to orchestrate the saving of the capital. The enemy assault began on 8 November. As 'defence supremo' Miaja proved a good delegator, adept at raising morale and in forging the will to resist the rebels at all costs. He was responsive to changing circumstances; thus, the command structure on the Madrid front was twice reorganized by the end of the year, with three mixed brigades to each of the five defence sectors. Miaja conducted an able joint leadership with Chief of Staff General Rojo, whose skilful planning helped to ensure initial success for the Republic's own offensives. He also played a key part in directing the civilian population in building a network of barricades and trenches. Controversy surrounds the organizational role played by General Goriev, the senior Russian adviser – highlighted by Hugh Thomas, but downplayed, as Thomas recognizes, by the Francoist Spanish historian Ricardo de la Cierva. Arguments have also occurred about Miaja and Rojo: Hills has suggested that General Rojo, when planning an offensive, did not always realistically evaluate the worth to the Republic of that specific terrain.

Turning from leaders to political parties, the historical consensus is that without the Spanish Communist Party (PCE), the defence of Madrid might have been much less efficient. The Party took a vigorous lead in fortifying the city and, influenced perhaps by Russian advisers, it conceived the innovatory idea of mixed brigades. The PCE offered exemplary training, and preached to an increasingly receptive audience the ethos of military discipline. The leading propagandist 'La Pasionaria', who exhorted resistance to the death, was not only leader of the Association of Antifascist Women but a member of the PCE Central Committee. Most battalion, brigade and divisional commanders on the Madrid front were also PCE, so it is hardly surprising that the Party came to dominate the Republican war effort. Furthermore, in the early months of the Civil War it had constructed the prestigious 'Fifth Regiment' of infantry – a model of discipline and training in up-to-date tactics. This bred a new generation of similar units but, again, has been held up to scrutiny. In *The Battle for Madrid* (1976), George Hills points to the Fifth Regiment's flagging counter-attack in the southern Madrid suburbs (November 1936) against the Nationalists' flank.[8] More significantly, however, the success of Russian tanks advancing ahead of the Fifth Regiment ended Nationalist hopes of outflanking Madrid from the south. Whatever the case, Fifth Regiment volunteers made up much of the early People's Army, and the latter's single chain of command and the mixed brigades added strength to the capital's defence.

Each of these mixed brigades was an autarkic whole: self-transporting and managing its own light artillery, sapper, ordnance and medical units. Colonel Galán's mixed brigade, for example, played a leading part in holding back the Nationalist advance west of Madrid in October–November 1936, while, in the Battle of Guadalajara in March 1937, the mixed brigades 'obeyed orders, operated coherently, and [showed] professional knowledge of tactics down to platoon and section level. They were an *army*.'[9]

Chapter 6 will offer further discussion of the International Brigades and the People's (Popular) Army. Here, however, it would be fitting to note the legendary status won by the IBs in all sectors in and around the capital. They raised morale and encouraged by example; played a key role in containing the Nationalist bridgehead in the west and north of Madrid, and helped maintain the Republicans' lines of communication; they led effective counter-attacks in January 1937 when the Nationalists tried to cut the Corunna Road west of the capital; and fought heroically at the Battle of the Jarama when the Nationalists similarly failed to cut the road to Valencia. The XIth and XIIth IBs routed the indisciplined 'volunteers' of Mussolini's CTV units north of Guadalajara (March 1937) and led a Republican breakthrough at Brunete four months later. Never had the term 'international community' contained such resonance.

To the west of Madrid, Republican forces had made the most of their strong defensive position and numerical advantage: it took the Nationalists a week to cross the River Manzanares, and by 22 November their attack had been contained. Crucially, successful rearguard defence had slowed down the rebel advance on Madrid in the autumn of 1936. It was, however, an inspired rearguard attack by government forces that disrupted the rebels' efforts to deploy their columns effectively. And, as Gabriel Jackson pointed out, with the IBs' strength of courage and of numbers, enemy strongholds in the University City were recaptured.[10]

In addition, the Republic had some of the best military equipment of the war. The USSR supplied top-quality T26 tanks with revolving turrets and higher speeds than the Italians' tankettes, while armoured cars used armour-piercing shells to knock out the light tanks supplied to Franco by Nazi Germany. From mid-November 1936 the Republic had more artillery at its disposal and by the end of the year calibres were being standardized (also those of rifles and machine-guns). Russian Polikarpov biplane and monoplane fighters confronted the Italian Fiats and German Heinkels and Messerschmitts, and at the Battle of Guadalajara the Republican air force was blessed with permanent runways. Until the summer of 1937 the Nationalists found it hard to break the Republic's daytime air superiority, and even when they did mount a terror bombing campaign they failed to break the will of the Madrileños. The capital also retained most of the detailed maps and their printing plates; as with the German army during the Anschluss, the Nationalists had to make do with motoring maps.

No less a reflection of Republican strength in the defence of Madrid were the weapons of propaganda and education. Icons of resistance such as 'La Pasionaria' and invocations to *stand fast* boosted both civilian and military resolve. But the rhetoric, in live speeches, Radio Madrid and the Republican press, was not monopolized by the PCE: the Socialists and anarchists also boasted powerful women orators such as Margarita Nelken and Federica Montseny. Furthermore, People's Army political commissars made hating the enemy, obedience and victory convincingly inseparable – even to anarchists. Michael Alpert, a leading authority on the Spanish army during this period, has written that these commissars were vital in convincing new recruits that victory was a pipedream without discipline and respect for competent authority.[11] At the Battle of Guadalajara the Republic won a propaganda coup when captured documents showed that the members of the Italian Corpo di Truppe Volontarie were in fact regular Italian army units and Fascist blackshirts.

Some mention should be made of the good fortune of the Republic and the weaknesses of its opponents. The wooded ground of the Casa de Campo (on the western outskirts of Madrid) was ideal for defence, and the rough ground in the Corunna Road campaign made coordination of the Nationalists' tank squadrons difficult. At the Battles of the Jarama and Guadalajara the weather benefited the Republic. In the former case, heavy rain delayed the Nationalist attack; in the latter, snow and ice halted Italian motorized columns, in any case low on fuel, and grounded Nationalist planes, including the Condor Legion. In his biography of Franco, Paul Preston brings into critical focus his personal role in the

Madrid sector: according to the author, Franco was indecisive and showed 'plodding, indeed hesitant, prudence'.[12] More broadly, the Republic held an advantage with regard to Nationalist leadership. At Guadalajara, for example, rivalry between Spanish Nationalist and Italian commanders undermined a westward advance on Madrid. Here again, Franco proved a blessing to the Republic for he appears to have used the less disciplined Italian forces to bear the worst of the Republican counter-attack while his own troops were rested and regrouped. Republican luck held when in early November 1936 the Nationalist assault plan against Madrid was found in an Italian tank. This allowed the Republican command to redeploy its forces accordingly and protect key bridges across the River Manzanares.

If the Republic could claim many strengths in the defence of Madrid, grave weaknesses were also evident. In the Madrid zone, criticism of individual commanders (Spanish and foreign) and disagreements between them soon came to the fore. Moreover, not only would focusing too closely on the defence of the capital distort the war effort; given its great advantages in resources, the Republic ran the risk of complacency. Rivalry between Generals Miaja and Pozas set back government forces at the Battle of the Jarama in February 1937. The Segovia Offensive, in May and June, failed to take pressure off Madrid: poor tactical leadership by the Polish general 'Walter' has been blamed. Following Franco's decision taken after Guadalajara to suspend further attacks on Madrid, political divisions grew in the Republican 'Defence Junta' between those who favoured 'revolution' and those who opposed it.

Indeed, politics intruded corrosively into the Republican war effort as, for example, Payne and Alpert have demonstrated. Thanks to the politically driven 'Committee of Investigation' set up in the summer of 1936 by the War Ministry, the talents of many able professional officers were not deployed in battle – a situation exacerbated by militia hostility to 'reactionary' professionals.[13] As described by Thomas and Preston, the death during the defence of Madrid's University City of anarchist leader Durruti led to bitter polemics between 'inefficient' anarchists and 'authoritarian' Communists, while Hills quotes President Azaña's desperate reference to 'indiscipline, anarchy, disorder, dissipation of time, energy and resources'.[14]

Late in July 1936, in the fighting for the three Guadarrama passes north of Madrid, official Republican reports berated the disobedience of militia troops which contributed to the rebels' successful capture of the Alta del León Pass. This left only one pass in government hands.

As has been seen, the PCE took the lead in improving militia training but, as Alpert has shown, the Republic suffered from a paucity of proper training schools.[15] This added dramatically to the evidence of weakness on the Republican side shown by the slow processing of conscripts. Deficiencies in air force training meant that Republican pilots were entering combat with inadequate flying hours behind them. Among junior army officers, inexperience and lack of initiative told badly against the Republic at the Battle of Brunete, west of Madrid, in July 1937. 'The failure of the Brunete offensive', asserts S.G. Payne, 'doomed the northern zone.'[16]

Brunete also revealed poor mobility on the part of Republican forces, described by Jackson as a failure to maintain momentum. The Republic found successful counter-offensives elusive: two in the outskirts of Madrid against the Nationalists' eastern flank failed in late October/early November 1936, partly due to poor coordination between tanks and infantry. These defective tactics were also shown at the Jarama (February 1937) when, as Esenwein and Shubert have observed, initial Republican gains were not consolidated. Soon after, at Guadalajara, Hills has the Republic failing to 'exploit their rout of the Italians' – although this 'rout' was a tremendous psychological and propaganda victory and Guadalajara, with its aircraft factory, remained in Republican hands.

Despite the positive evidence discussed earlier, the weapons in the hands of the Republic could prove, to say the least, problematical. The French Dewoitine fighter aircraft had poor engines; later models bought from the Lithuanian government had, where feasible, to be armed from scratch in Spain. Foreign individuals and governments, for example the Polish, harvested vast sums of money in cynical or desperate deals.[17] Meanwhile, as Hugh Thomas has suggested, the Nationalists' new CR32 biplane often proved an unexpected match for its Republican Polikarpov counterpart, as in a memorable dogfight over Madrid on 13 November 1936. And the Republic had no nightfighters to parry Condor Legion bombers when they launched their night raids on the city, nor adequate anti-aircraft cover. Both sides, however, suffered from unreliable bomb-sights and ground-to-air communications. At the beginning of the Civil War, the Republican forces were making do with obsolete rifles from Germany, Mexico, and, via Russia, Swiss designs from the 1860s; while it could be that three out of four guns in an artillery troop had different calibres (altogether there were nine different artillery calibres in use). Preston has drawn a depressing picture of how all these armaments were paid for: if Russian, by the shipment of the gold reserve to Moscow; too often otherwise, on the cut-throat international arms market where exorbitant charges were made for antiquated weapons.[18]

Nevertheless, the defence of Madrid represented a heroic exercise in mobilization, both military and civilian. It demonstrated resilience and resolve; the fighting in the University City was indeed a ferocious battle of minds. Resistance to Nationalist attack offered objective evidence of Republican success: despite flaws in organization and resources, despite massive casualties, government forces contained the rebel bridgehead. Major roads out of the capital were kept open. What is ironic, however, is that the strength of Madrid proved a weakness for the Republic, for it encouraged the Nationalists to focus their strength on weaker sectors elsewhere. The humiliation of the Italian CTV at Guadalajara made Mussolini determined to fight on until Franco had won. Thus, in these senses, 'strengths and weaknesses' were inseparable.

Questions

1. What was the significance of individual political and military leaders in the 'Battle for Madrid'?
2. How successful was the defence of Madrid?

SOURCES

REVOLUTION IN THE REPUBLICAN ZONE?

Source A: from *Adelante*, a PSOE newspaper published in Valencia, 1 May 1937.

At the outbreak of the Fascist revolt the labour organizations and the democratic elements in the country were in agreement that the so-called Nationalist Revolution, which threatened to plunge our people into an abyss of deepest misery, could be halted only by a Social Revolution. The Communist Party, however, opposed this view with all its might. It had apparently completely forgotten its old theories of a 'workers' and peasants' republic' and a 'dictatorship of the proletariat'. From its constant repetition of its new slogan of the parliamentary democratic republic it is clear that it has lost all sense of reality. When the Catholic and conservative sections of the Spanish bourgeoisie saw their old system smashed and could find no way out, the Communist Party instilled new hope into them. It assured them that the democratic bourgeois republic for which it was pleading put no obstacles in the way of Catholic propaganda and, above all, that it stood ready to defend the class interests of the bourgeoisie.

Source B: Santiago Carrillo, of the Central Committee of the PCE, on fighting for a democratic Republic.

We are fighting against Fascism, against foreign intruders, but we are not today fighting for a socialist revolution. There are people who tell us that we must come out for a socialist revolution and there are those who proclaim that our fight for the democratic republic is only a pretext to conceal our real purposes. No, we are not carrying out any tactical manoeuvre, nor have we any kind of concealed intentions against the Spanish government and world democracy. We are fighting with complete sincerity for the democratic republic ... Any other attitude would not only favour the victory of the Fascist intruders, it would even contribute to the transplanting of Fascism into the remaining bourgeois–democratic states.

Source C: from *Homage to Catalonia* by George Orwell, 1938.

[The] Spanish working class did not, as we might conceivably do in England, resist Franco in the name of 'democracy' and the *status quo*; their resistance was accompanied by – one might almost say it consisted of – a definite revolutionary outbreak. Land was seized by the peasants; many factories and most of the transport were seized by the trade unions; churches were wrecked and the priests driven out or killed. The *Daily Mail*, amid the cheers of the Catholic clergy, was able to represent Franco as a patriot delivering his country from hordes of fiendish 'Reds' ...

Even if one had heard nothing of the seizure of the land by the peasants, the setting up of local soviets, etc., it would be hard to believe that the Anarchists and Socialists who were the backbone of the resistance were doing this kind of thing for the preservation of capitalist democracy, which especially in the Anarchist view was no more than a centralised swindling machine.

Source D: Gaston Leval, a French anarchist, writes about collectives, 1938.

The agrarian revolution has inaugurated the practice of Libertarian right. And it has done it with such results that the Anarchist theorists themselves, those who had always defended the concepts now applied, were amazed, and will never forget the beautiful dream through which they lived ...

In about three months, most of the villages of Aragon, some of which were wrested from Fascist hands by the columns led by Durruti and other 'undisciplined' guerillas, organized agrarian collectives. One must not confuse the industrial 'collectives' carried out under the aegis of the decree mentioned earlier on, and under instructions dictated by the Catalan Government, with those of the peasants. This word 'collectives' describes two quite different things.

The mechanism of the formation of the Aragonese collectives, has been generally the same. After having overcome the local authorities when they were fascist, or after having replaced them by Anti-fascist or Revolutionary committees when they were not, an assembly was summoned for all the inhabitants of the locality to decide on their line of action.

Source E: from *The Villages are the Heart of Spain* by American author John Dos Passos, 1937.

Some of [the nobles] were shot, others managed to get away. The Casa del Pueblo [the local HQ of the Socialist Party/UGT] formed a collective out of their lands. Meanwhile other lands were taken over by the CNT local . . . The Casa del Pueblo, having the majority of the working farmers, took over the municipal government and it was decided that every working man should be paid five pesetas for every day he worked and have a right to a daily litre of wine and a certain amount of firewood. The mayor and the secretary and treasurer and the muledrivers and the blacksmith, every man who worked was paid the same. The carpenters and masons and other skilled artisans who had been making seven pesetas a day consented, gladly they said, to taking the same pay as the rest. Later, the mastermason told me, they'd raise everybody's pay to seven pesetas or higher; after all wine was a valuable crop and with no parasites to feed there would be plenty for all. Women and boys were paid three fifty. The committees of the UGT and the CNT decided every day where their members were to work. Housing was roughly distributed according to the sizes of the families.

Questions

1. Explain the references to: (a) bourgeois–democratic states (Source B); (b) Durruti (Source D). (2)
2. What are the main differences between the arguments and language used by the authors of Sources A and B? (4)
3. To what extent are the arguments expressed in Source B reinforced by the observations in Source C? (4)
*4. What are the advantages and disadvantages of Sources D and E for a historian studying collectivization in Republican Spain? (7)
5. Using these sources and your own knowledge, discuss the view that, on the Republican side in the Spanish Civil War, 'revolution was a deeply divisive issue'. (8)

Worked answer

*4. [You might plan this answer by making a table of 'Advantages' and 'Disadvantages' from the two sources. Your further reading may enable you to validate what each states.]

In Aragón, the primary focus of Source D, there were about 450 collectives, some of the most thoroughly researched in Spain. The Frenchman Gaston Leval, author of this source, was a pioneering first-hand witness. His language, especially in the first paragraph (and the critical use of inverted commas in the second paragraph), reflects his own deep commitment to the anarchist cause. For a balanced evaluation of collectivization one would therefore need to look further afield. However, Leval reliably describes the circumstances in which Aragón collectives were established, and a significant contrast is made between what Leval sees as 'dictated' and 'democratic' collectives. Also requiring evaluation would be Leval's reference (first paragraph) to 'such results'. Moreover, in Source D there is no sense of change through time, although elsewhere Leval does allude to the attack on collectives made by the Communists in 1937 – a process completed in Aragón by Franco's Nationalists in 1938. (A 'fundamental law' of the Communists and their supporters was that defeating fascism was *the* priority: collectivization would not win the war.)

In Source E, Dos Passos provides his own personal profile of Fuentidueña, a village east of Madrid which featured in the film *The Spanish Earth*. Insights offered in Source E include: the role and powers of the Casa del Pueblo; the inference that the Municipal Council continued to exist (also evident elsewhere); that there were *two* collectives, one UGT and one CNT, and that there was a modus vivendi between the two; that they were general village collectives, rather than just agricultural; that money continued to exist (in some collectives it was abolished); and that, in practice, egalitarianism fell short. Thus women were paid less than men. Dos Passos does not spell out why, nor is it clear how the collectives' wages stood compared to the rest of Madrid Province or Spain as a whole. (In fact, collective wages for working couples in the Madrid area were the highest in Spain.)

Both Sources D and E provide primary evidence of collectivization in Spain. However, further research would be needed on, for example, increases or decreases in production, industrial collectives and how opposition to collectives expressed itself. Both Sources D and E refer to the violence which preceded collectivization ('wrested'; 'overcome'; 'shot'), but neither to the coercion which sometimes accompanied it nor the anti-collective organizations supported by the PCE, PSUC and Catalan Esquerra (Left) Party.

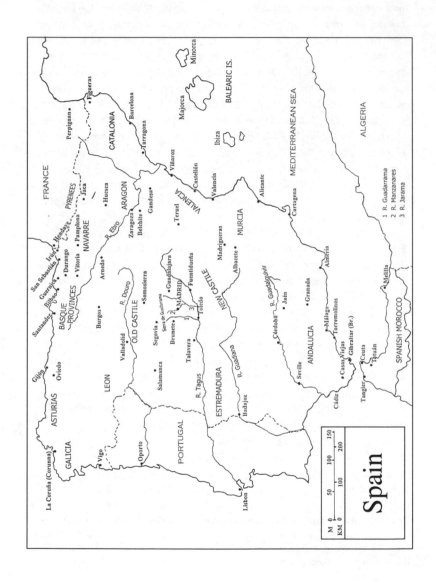

Spain

Figure 1 All youth united for the Fatherland. A poster issued in Valencia by
the Propaganda Secretariat of the Juventudes Socialistas Unificadas (JSU).
c. 100 × 70 cm.
Source: V & A Picture Library

Figure 2 KULTUR! Fascist barbarism in Madrid. A poster issued by the Propaganda Section of the CNT-AIT National Committee and published in several language editions. c. 100 × 70 cm.

Source: V & A Picture Library

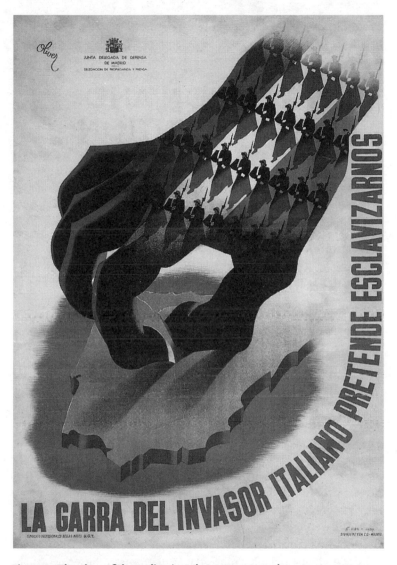

Figure 3 The claw of the Italian invader grasps to enslave us. A poster
issued by the Madrid Defence Junta (Propaganda and Press Branch), 1937.
c. 100 × 70 cm.
Source: V & A Picture Library

5

INTERVENTION AND NON-INTERVENTION: IDEALISM OR EXPEDIENCY?

BACKGROUND NARRATIVE

Not long after the abortive Nationalist coup in mid-July 1936 it became evident that the Spanish Civil War – despite its origins in indigenous conflicts – would be more than a domestic Spanish affair. Such things were not new: in Russia between 1918 and 1921 'interventions' had sought to change the government, without success. But in Spain two decades later, intervention (and non-intervention) by foreign powers, whether deliberately or by default, saw to it that the government did change.

To see the Spanish Civil War in its full international perspective, its impact on the intervening and 'neutral' powers (and relations between them) needs to be considered. For example, the war further weakened Italy's economy and was instrumental in forging the Rome–Berlin Axis. It led to splits in the French and British cabinets and eventually to Anthony Eden's resignation as Foreign Secretary. In the United States it helped undermine the isolationist consensus. (The significance of Russian intervention and of the International Brigades is considered in detail in the next chapter.)

On several levels, 1936 set the pattern for future developments. Having decided to assist the insurgents, Hitler and Mussolini supplied

Junkers and Savoia-Marchetti aircraft to transport the Spanish Foreign Legion and Moorish *regulares* from Morocco. Heinkel biplane fighters were landed at Cádiz by early August 1936 and, though towards the end of the month Germany and Italy 'agreed in principle' to non-intervention, up to October 1936 freighters regularly left German ports loaded with combat aircraft, artillery and light tanks. From August, too, Italian fighter planes flew missions in Spain. The first bombing raids on Madrid took place on 28 August. Portugal had also pledged assistance to the Nationalists. American Texaco oil helped fuel the latter's war effort from the first weeks of the conflict; American motor companies such as Ford supplied Franco's forces with trucks.

In France the question of whether to support the Spanish Republican government divided the Popular Front cabinet of Léon Blum. In fact, nearly fifty French biplanes (Neuport-Delage 52s) built in Spain were already in use by government forces in July 1936; by mid-October a further ninety-four French aircraft had been delivered to Spain. However, non-intervention became the official stance, as the best means of 'quarantining' the conflict.

In early August Britain and France produced a draft policy proposal, though when the Non-Intervention Committee held its first meeting in London in early September interventionist powers were, ironically, at least as conspicuous by their presence as Britain, France and the Soviet Union. (Until mid-October, Russian aid to the Republic consisted mainly of food.) Not surprisingly, Republican Spain's efforts to present its case to the Non-Intervention Committee, and the League of Nations, many of whose members were pro-Franco, yielded nothing positive.

October 1936 proved a crucial month. Responding to the Republicans' deteriorating position, Soviet Russia began some deliveries of military aid. Nazi Germany and Fascist Italy therefore decided to intensify their own assistance to the Nationalist side, whose credit on Texaco oil was also guaranteed at this time. Portugal had already formalized its direct military aid to Franco by creating the Portuguese Legion. The German Condor Legion arrived by sea in November; German advisers were already in Madrid to assist the Nationalist commander General Varela. By early December, Italy had supplied over 100 aircraft, as well as small tanks, artillery and machine-guns; before Christmas the port of Cádiz welcomed the first Italian 'volunteers', nearly 50,000 of whom were to land by February, in time to suffer ignominious defeat at the Battle of Guadalajara. Germany's and Italy's diplomatic recognition of Franco as Spanish Head of State in November 1936 had given them spurious grounds for arguing that they were now merely helping the government.

Meanwhile, Britain and France adhered officially to non-intervention, except for the occasional reopening of the French border when the state of French politics permitted. They appeared to take a stronger line against arms imports to Spain through the British Merchant Shipping Act (December 1936) and Non-Intervention Committee sea patrols (April 1937). However, the September 1937 Nyon Agreement to sink 'pirate', that is, Italian, submarines only came into effect after Italian submarine attacks had ended. Having initially sought to prevent the passage of arms to Spain, in February 1937 the Non-Intervention Committee extended the ban, with no more success, to foreign volunteers. Despite morale-boosting temporary gains, for example, at Teruel in southern Aragón and in the Ebro Valley (in early and mid-1938, respectively), over 2 million dollars' worth of arms from Mexico, and international outrage at the destruction of Guernica in April 1937, the Republic continued to lose territory – notably in the south and north in 1937 and then in 1938 (faced with yet more German and Italian aid to Franco) in the east. A new American Neutrality Act in May 1937 indirectly strengthened Franco's position and his eventual victory in the Ebro Valley (November 1938) was, in military terms, decisive.

How might a compromise peace between Republican and Nationalist forces – a dwindling hope of Negrín's Republican government – be achieved? By the withdrawal of all foreign volunteers? Whatever the case, international attention was switching to central Europe. Wider diplomatic considerations were already intervening in April 1938 when a reference to 'substantial withdrawal' of Italian troops from Spain formed part of the 'Anglo-Italian Agreement'. In the months after the German Anschluss, the Czech crisis reached boiling point. The Munich Agreement of 29 September, in which Britain and France yielded to Hitler's demand for the Sudetenland, 'was a death blow to the diplomatic hopes of the Spanish Republic'.[1] Stalin now realized that he might have to 'deal' with a dangerously aggrandizing Nazi Reich. A price for this would – ironically – be appeasement, namely withdrawing from Spain the anti-fascist International Brigades, whose farewell parades took place at the end of October 1938. However, the Condor Legion and troops from the Italian CTV remained in Spain until May 1939, several weeks after Franco's victory. The extent of Franco's own non-interventionism in the Second World War was yet to be revealed.

ANALYSIS (1): WHAT WAS THE SIGNIFICANCE OF GERMAN AID TO THE NATIONALIST SIDE?

Some of the reasons for Nazi Germany and Fascist Italy's intervention in the events in Spain from July 1936 were touched on briefly in the two previous chapters. What seems clear, however, is that a Nazi and Italian Fascist presence did not so much start the conflict as play a major role in sustaining it, manipulating and redefining it, and in determining its outcome: in Spain, victory for Franco; abroad, a deepening gulf (with significant qualifications) between fascist and anti-fascist powers. This analysis will focus principally on the significance of German aid to what, not so long after the initiation of hostilities, could be called 'Franco Spain'.

Vitally important in its timing, Operation Magic Fire conveyed troops of the Army of Africa – reputedly the best in the Spanish army – to the mainland. Denis Smyth has written of the 'isolation and piecemeal defeat' of the insurgents that would have occurred had the airlifts not taken place.[2] Christian Leitz draws attention to a highly significant strategic gain which German transport soon made possible – namely, the Nationalists' capture of Badajoz close to the Portuguese border, which assured access to Lisbon, the port which became a major docking-point for high-quality German *matériel*.[3]

These weapons were to play a decisive role in helping the Nationalists to win what was, after all, an unexpected civil war. Admittedly, their effectiveness could not be taken for granted. For example, most aircraft initially lacked radio sets. However, by mid-1937 German successes had helped to reassert Nationalist air superiority. On the ground, the use of German triple-function (artillery, anti-tank and anti-aircraft) 88mm guns and MG34 machine-guns proved hard to match. However, as Alpert observes, without German naval patrols to protect the (disguised) arms-carrying ships, the *matériel* might never have arrived – nor the Republican naval lifelines been squeezed.[4] Moreover, by the end of October 1936

Hitler authorized a significant expansion of Germany's aid programme, for he saw that the Spanish conflict would not be a 'short war' and he was determined neither to be outshone by Mussolini nor to allow the Russian aid now pouring in to swing the balance away from Franco's Nationalists.

The Condor Legion came to personify this new phase of German aid to those forces working to reinstate 'traditional Spanish values'. The legion's help was conditional: the Nationalists must try harder to win the war and accept German command of this force. Partly experimental, it was, in P.M.H. Bell's words, a 'compact and efficient body' whose contribution was 'out of all proportion to its size'.[5] Research in the late 1980s by American historian Robert Whealey revealed that only about 5,500 CL personnel were based in Spain at any one time. Predictably, however, for Hitler it was the CL and its chief of staff von Richtofen who were the architects of Franco's victory.

The CL first saw action over Cartagena and Madrid in November 1936. South of the capital, at the Battle of the Jarama, the 88mm guns first saw action, their lethal accuracy restricting the air-support role of the Republican air force. To maximize the use of its own well-maintained combat planes and their equally well-trained crews, companies of air-communications specialists were also provided. The Condor Legion's support ensured the collapse of the defensive 'iron ring' around Bilbao which fell on 7 June 1937. This key development put naval shipyards as well as more iron, steel and artillery shell production in Franco's hands (Mola had been killed four days before); and now there were no cableheads left in Republican hands, strengthening Franco's grip on communications. As Preston has shown, the Germans masterminded this Vizcayan campaign, though it was not until late August 1937 that, east of Santander, the Basque army finally yielded.[6]

Inexorably, the Nationalists advanced west on the Asturias, where the Condor Legion used primitive napalm to subvert Republican morale. The fall of the Asturias was in some ways more signficant than that of Bilbao, for now coordination of Asturian coal and Basque iron ore production could in turn feed the munitions factories. Furthermore, local conscription swelled the ranks of the Nationalist armies for future campaigns.[7] Beginning in December 1937, the eastern campaign would eventually split in two what remained of the Republic.

Already at Brunete the value of the new Messerschmitt 109 monoplane fighter had been demonstrated: the Nationalists achieved, and would not yield, air superiority in the central theatre. Now, following Franco's successful recapture in February 1938 of Teruel in southern Aragón – thanks partly to CL aircover – thirty-six of these cutting-edge aircraft, along with 200 tanks, were deployed in the offensive which would take Franco's forces north to the French border. Simultaneously, in the Nationalists' march east to the sea, over 1,000 German and Italian planes saw action, though such impressive numbers were offset by disagreements over tank tactics and by France's allowing Republican supplies across the border into Spain. Nevertheless, by mid-April 1938 the Nationalists had reached the eastern coast.

The subsequent Ebro Valley Campaign between July and November 1938 began as a Republican offensive but ultimately positioned the Nationalists for their final thrust in Catalonia. Here, the Condor Legion again proved significant. Indeed, as Thomas, Smyth and Preston have suggested, the two waves of CL reinforcements and delivery of new German equipment, in return for mining concessions, reinvigorated the Nationalist forces for their success on the Ebro and final push on Barcelona.[8]

If the Condor Legion symbolized Nazi intervention, then Guernica, which in Picasso's painting would become the hell of war as art form, expressed the full horror of Nazi military tactics in Spain. On 26 April 1937, as a result of 185 minutes' bombing, the market town was left a smouldering and bloody skeleton – an act of grotesque perfection by over fifty aircraft of the Condor Legion and Italian Aviazione Legionaria. Although as a communications base and escape hatch for retreating Republican Basques the town was a military target, Guernica was also part of Mola's plan to destroy the morale of the Vizcayan population and thus wipe out their will to resist. But submission was not forthcoming: the Basque army fought on for four months. Furthermore, because of the particular brutality of this assault and the fact that thousands of Basque children were welcomed abroad as refugees, Guernica permanently raised the war's international profile.

This can be seen to exemplify the 'wider contribution' of Nazi intervention, but within Spain the role of pro-Nationalist German personnel (estimates vary from 10,000 to 16,000) went beyond that of direct combat. Many were instructors or communications experts. The battleship *Deutschland* had among its crew signals specialists to help Franco intercept Republican merchant shipping.

The Third Reich's contribution to the Nationalist war effort was valued by Hugh Thomas at 540 million Reichsmarks, of which the Condor Legion cost 354 million.[9] How was it all to be paid for? HISMA/ROWAK operated the symbiotic connection between the Spanish Nationalist war machine and the German war economy. Franco needed German *matériel* right through to the winter of 1938 and beyond; Germany needed Spanish raw materials to offset the export of military hardware to Franco and to fuel its own rearmament programme. These links represented a very narrow economic corridor for Franco's foreign exchange; they also excluded many business interests within Germany.

Christian Leitz, a leading expert on economic relations between Germany and Spain whose researches in Germany include the Federal Archive in Koblenz, has presented a clear and concise analysis of HISMA/ROWAK and its significance. As he explains, the original function of HISMA, from its first base in Spanish Morocco, was to arrange the carriage of Franco's troops and equipment. A later branch of HISMA was set up in Bilbao, the leading source of iron ore: HISMA's additional, and thereafter central, role was to process Franco's debt repayments in the form of raw materials. Apart from iron ore and pyrites (for explosives), these included zinc, tin and tungsten, all of which were required by IGFarben-werke, Germany's leading chemical conglomerate. ROWAK was HISMA's twin company, operating as the import distributor in Germany and locking in to the 'massive exploitation of Franco's dependence on German military and economic aid', forwarding these Spanish minerals to industrial plants in the Ruhr.[10]

Beyond such interdependent military and economic considerations, what else was significant about German aid to the Nationalists? It certainly gave a vivid insight into Germany's wider perceptions of Europe. A Spanish Nationalist victory could divide France's forces in time of war by burdening it with the defence of a second front. It could also block the passage of French colonial troops by sea and land. France was also allied to Russia: therefore, it was vital to defeat the Spanish Republic which might have aligned with a Franco-Russian 'axis' and reinforced Germany's encirclement by foreign powers. As Denis Smyth has put it, 'Prevention was the mother of intervention.'[11] German hopes for Britain were somewhat contradictory: seduced by the Führer's relentless assault on Bolshevism in Spain, 'England' would favour Germany and distance itself from 'passive' France; on the other hand, a Franco victory could disrupt the British navy. Italy (and the other powers) must be diverted from central Europe, where Germany's expansionist policies were soon to enter a more dynamic and dangerous phase. The Axis, however, must be sustained, for it was the 'new arbiter' in European affairs. Another aspect of keeping Italy involved in Spain was to get it to play the larger part in feeding Franco's war machine. For Germany did not want to incite France to an anti-German war by unrestricted Wehrmacht assaults on the Spanish Republic.

However, German aid to Franco would serve both the Wehrmacht and the Luftwaffe well. At the Hossbach Conference in November 1937 Hitler contemplated war in Europe; Spain provided a combat environment in which weapons and tactics could be tested and refined. For example, two advanced monoplane fighter aircraft were tried out. The Heinkel 112 was sent for experimental missions, but it was the Messerschmitt 109 that proved the more impressive. In the Spanish arena at least four variants of the Messerschmitt were put through their paces, and tactics in aerial combat were developed and established. The campaigns in Vizcaya and the Asturias baptized the 'flying pencil' – the new Dornier 17 bomber which was faster than the Heinkel 111s – and Junkers 87 divebombers which were to become the screaming scourge of Poland in 1939 and of France in 1940.

Yet recriminations peppered the relationship between Germany and the Nationalists. The haughty General Faupel, the Reich's first ambassador to Franco, was a notorious meddler and extremely unpopular. Conversely, German (and Italian) aid frustrated its donors because Franco seemed to be manipulating it to pursue his own slow agenda of near-genocidal attrition against the 'reds'. His enemies could then be consigned to the dustbin of history.

Among historians, subjects for debate have included the economic dimension, and the obliteration of Guernica. Were economic advantages of intervening in Spain a 'by-product' (Smyth) or did they 'loom large' (Alpert) in Germany's thinking?[12] Who was responsible for the Guernica atrocity? Was it the Basques themselves aiming to reap a propaganda advantage that, in a tragically ironic sense, they achieved anyway? Or was it the Francoist hierarchy releasing the Condor Legion over Guernica with orders to kill the spirit of Basque resistance and open the way to Bilbao twenty kilometres to the west? In his seminal 1977 dissection, 'Guernica! Guernica!' A Study of Journalism, Diplomacy, Propaganda and History, Herbert R. Southworth has shown the latter to have been the case.

In conclusion, thanks to intervention by Nazi Germany and Fascist Italy, and despite or because of the Non-Intervention Committee, the Spanish Civil War became a war about international fascism. But how universal and how durable was the conviction with which this war was waged? It has been said that the intervention kept the war going but that the extent of German aid was calculated to prevent a general war. Even so, military success in Spain compensated for Hitler's frustration over the Sudetenland in September 1938. It also formed the technical and tactical precedent for the German triumphs of 1939 and 1940. Historians have also argued that Germany and Italy did not try to impose political influence on Franco as Stalin had done over the Republicans. But Hitler and Mussolini did not need to wield this control, for there was a much greater meeting of minds, and there were few internal divisions on the Nationalist side to fracture their military and economic conduct of the war. Finally, German and Italian aid (and British and French non-intervention) forced the Soviet Union to shore up the Republic. In turn, the Third Reich and Fascist Italy, partners in an anti-communist crusade, cemented the Rome–Berlin Axis, which paved the way for the Pact of Steel in May 1939 and Italy's intervention in the Second World War thirteen unlucky months later. In 1940 both Hitler and Mussolini would themselves experience humiliating failures; in the Battle of Britain and invasions of Greece and Egypt, respectively. Hitler's attention then focused on the Soviet Union and detailed planning of the ill-fated Operation Barbarossa. It would be Franco's turn, via the Falangist Blue Division, to support Hitler, to show his gratitude in blood for the Führer's help in defeating Bolshevism in Spain.

Questions

1. 'The Condor Legion was but one aspect of Nazi Germany's intervention in the Spanish Civil War.' Discuss.
2. How significant was Italian Fascist intervention in the Spanish Civil War?

ANALYSIS (2): WHY, AND WITH WHAT SUCCESS, DID BRITAIN AND FRANCE ADOPT A POLICY OF NON-INTERVENTION?

This question in turn begs others: What is meant by Britain and France? By non-intervention? By success? As will be seen, 'Britain and France' cannot be defined here as one entity pursuing a singular goal. 'Success' can be evaluated with regard to Britain and France themselves; to other powers (persuading them, or not, to keep out); and to Spain itself. As for 'non-intervention', W. Foss and C. Gerahty, writing at the height of the Civil War, described it by defining its opposite: 'Any assistance of any kind given to either side in a war is intervention.' But in the context of the Spanish Civil War non-intervention could, paradoxically, be just as interventionist, and just as decisive.

In its official policy of non-intervention, the British government was intensely pragmatic. Baldwin, Prime Minister 1935–7, was seeking a structured co-existence between the states of Europe: war in Spain was an irritating tangent. Chamberlain, his successor, baulked at a confrontation with interventionist Italy: Mussolini must be prised from his Axis partner Hitler, not welded closer to him by a hostile Britain. This pragmatism extended to Spain itself, where Britain's economic and strategic concerns should not be undermined by supporting the side that might lose the Civil War. The chiefs of staff stressed the urgent imperial commitments of Britain's armed forces in the Far East and elsewhere, and wondered if it was necessary to intervene against Franco. Drawing on the evidence of contemporary meetings and reports, the Spanish historian Enrique Moradiellos notes how the Caudillo presented to British officials the image of a conservative nationalist posing no threat to British investment, trade or strategic interests.[13] Moreover, was it desirable to help the Republic? In these same interviews Franco stressed he had merely done his patriotic duty in rising up against anarchy and social revolution. Indeed, most politicians in Baldwin's National Government thought it best to steer well clear of a 'Scarlet Spain' that was likely to be pro-Russian and potentially infectious. As First Lord of the Admiralty Sir Samuel Hoare put it, if Bolshevism spread to Portugal Britain's imperial lifelines would be in grave danger. Pro-Franco groups in Britain such as the Anglo-German Fellowship reinforced this anti-communist message.

France was a crucial element in these calculations. Blum's Popular Front government must be discouraged from aiding Popular Front Spain: a Paris–Madrid Axis might be even worse than Rome–Berlin. And the scenario of an Anglo-French alliance with Soviet Russia in the Spanish cockpit was contemplated with horror. Such developments could only encourage international revolution and, furthermore, exacerbate German fears of encirclement. The goal remained European appeasement and stability, not confrontation and war.

In fact, France itself was deeply divided over Spain, both within the Popular Front government and among the populace. As distilled by Anthony Adamthwaite, an authority on France's external relations, 'Foreign policy, an integrating force before 1914, became a source of division.'[14] Socialist Prime Minister Blum's instincts were to help the Spanish Republic, but not all in his Popular Front coalition shared his sympathies. Blum's second thoughts were confirmed by a ruthless attack on him from the right-wing press in Paris and pressure on him from Britain to be 'prudent'. At a Socialist rally in September 1936 Blum explained the agonizing dilemma he faced, but added that he had a duty to France as a whole. Turning to Spain itself, and to Europe, he declared, 'If we send [arms] other countries will help the rebels . . . Even for Spain it is better to have an international agreement which would benefit the Spanish government . . . Non-intervention has probably already avoided a European war.'[15]

In any case, France's depression was proving woefully stubborn, with industrial production falling by 24 per cent between 1929 and

1938. Militarily, France was distracted by rebellions in North Africa. Diplomatically, as with Britain, Italian support was being cultivated in order to break the Axis connection. France also sought an economic and colonial agreement with Germany to strengthen moderate opinion there. And if France intervened directly in Spain and confronted Italy and Germany there, she risked not only international war but a civil war in France itself, with the prospect of a reactionary right-wing government rising from the ashes.

Blum had recognized that if France sent arms to the Spanish Republic then other countries would help the (Nationalist) rebels. As Anthony Eden, Chamberlain's foreign secretary, could see only too clearly, other states, specifically Italy and Germany, were indeed aiding the rebels. Britain's faith had been placed in Franco to secure Britain's interests. But Franco had not been blessed with an easy victory and the British government feared that the Axis powers would so entrench themselves on the Nationalist side that they would dictate an anti-British policy. Thus, Eden tried to confront the dictators with a firmer non-intervention policy, for example a blockade of Axis ships bound for Spain. But Chamberlain, pursuing the diametrically opposed policy of conciliation, would not go that far. In disgust, Eden resigned in February 1938 over what he saw as Chamberlain's pusillanimous attitude to Hitler's and Mussolini's Spanish intervention.

So much for the British Foreign Secretary's own 'success' in trying to buttress the non-intervention policy. More broadly, how successful was non-intervention as pursued by Britain and France? In Britain, the policy could claim a wide basis of support. For at least a year, national government and Labour Party leaders maintained a bipartisan policy of non-intervention. In contrasting ways, two prominent Labour figures illustrate this position: Hugh Dalton argued not only that it took two sides to make a war – the Republic itself was not blameless – but that Britain's own rearmament programme would be blown off course by an 'arms to Spain' policy; while Ernest Bevin (later one of the founders of NATO as a deterrent to war) forcefully warned of world war should military non-intervention be thrown overboard.[16] Labour pro-interventionists could not undermine this implacably non-interventionist line, which was shared by right-wing leaders of the Trades Union Council.

Even when the Labour Party and TUC officially abandoned non-intervention at their 1937 conferences in the face of the horrific evidence emerging from Spain, the government's non-interventionist policy, supported by *The Times* and other influential broadsheets, held fast. In Chamberlain's eyes, Franco commanded a cohesive, conservative movement. Surely he would seek British economic help and respect

Britain's interests. Similarly in France, despite some goodwill to the Spanish Republic in the form of 'relaxed' non-intervention, undiluted non-intervention remained the French government's public stance. French Communist Party attempts to force it through strike action to embrace a 'guns and planes for Spain' policy failed. This does not mean that the Popular Front did nothing. But, as Michael Alpert has observed, to avoid provoking the French into all-out support for the Spanish Republic, both Germany and Italy joined the Non-Intervention Committee.[17] Once they, barely concealing their cynicism, had taken their stance, so also did Soviet Russia 'adhere'; in formal terms at least, this was another criterion for non-intervention's 'success'.

With respect to more tangible policy achievements, attempts were made to strengthen non-intervention. A Non-Intervention Naval Patrol came into effect in April 1937. Following an international agreement, signed at Nyon in Switzerland, to act against 'unidentified pirate' (code for 'Italian') submarines, further patrols began in September of that year. These continued until August 1938, at which point they were declared 'successful'. At last the Non-Intervention Committee had been seen to take a stand. However, evasion of both these initiatives proved even more skilful. Despite the Naval Patrol, smuggling was rife: vessels flew Panamanian or other non-agreement flags, or they had warship 'minders'. Spanish ships were exempt anyway, even if delivering arms from Soviet Russia. And Mussolini outflanked the Nyon Agreement by transferring his submarines directly to Franco and his offensive against pro-Republic shipping to the air.

The Non-Intervention Agreement, and the committee designed to uphold it, lacked muscle. The agreement was not binding in international law; accusations of contravention were hermetically sealed inside the committee, which conveniently excluded Spain. But if Italy and Germany could continue to provision the Nationalist war effort, it is also evident that supplies for the Republic reached their destination. The International Brigades (examined in the next chapter) were organized from Paris and France further compromised its own non-intervention policy. It allowed private arms sales and permitted Republican planes to use French airspace. In addition, specially selected customs officials organized the smuggling of *matériel* into the Republican zone; the customs apparatus was short-circuited by false documents, disguised shipments, and 'third party' devices – for example, Romania sending wheat to Spain via France in return for French goods.[18] Writing in 1938, the right-wing journalists W. Foss and C. Gerahty 'explained' French intervention as part of an international plot by Freemasons. Quoting from such ultra-nationalist French newspapers as *L'Action Française*, they sought to quantify war *matériel* sent to the Spanish Republic long after the signing of the Non-Intervention Agreement in August 1936. Foss and Gerahty had an axe to grind and their sources were dubious, but the evidence for French involvement nevertheless stands up.

France's *de facto* involvement added pressure on Nazi Germany to aid Franco, so that the success of non-intervention was further undermined. How did non-government organizations in Britain take the initiative in helping the Republic and, to a lesser extent, the Nationalists? Tom Buchanan's extensive archival research has detailed the work of the many British aid programmes active during the Spanish Civil War.[19] There were also notable aid initiatives in other countries, for example, the United States, as Esenwein and Shubert have described in *Spain at War* (1995). In Britain the Spanish Workers' Fund gave generously to the Republican cause. The National Joint Committee for Spanish Relief, in which the dissident Tory 'Red Kitty' (Duchess of) Atholl played a prominent part, spent most of its funds caring for Spanish children in the Republican zone. The Spanish Medical Aid Committee worked in Republican hospitals; the Quakers' Friends Service Council provided ambulance units. The moral case for intervention over the Nationalists' siege of Bilbao seemed watertight. Here, state and independent initiatives collaborated together: with private vessels protected by Royal Navy destroyers such as *Havoc* and the battlecruiser *Hood*, attempts were made to break Franco's blockade of the northern coast. Meanwhile, the pro-Franco Bishops' Committee for the Relief of Spanish Distress was launched by leading Roman Catholics to help the Nationalist side, and fund-raising campaigns were begun by Catholic newspapers such as *The Tablet*. However, 'The image of Nationalist Spain was not one which combined easily with humanitarian aid . . . the Nationalists were [seen as] martial and aggressively self-reliant.'[20]

In conclusion, such initiatives might not have turned the tide of the Spanish Civil War in either direction, but were, it might be claimed, more impressive than the work of the Non-Intervention Committee. It is true that there was no civil war in France and that the war in Spain did not produce the feared immediate 'domino effect' in the rest of Europe. But if, for the British government at least, 'non-intervention' was a covert way first of helping Franco to win in the expectation that he would lead an enlightened dictatorship and be pro-British and second of maintaining a line to Italy in order to detach the Duce from the Axis, it failed on both counts. And, despite the hope that non-intervention would contain the conflict, in some senses the Spanish Civil War did indeed lead in the longer term to a European war. The Axis was born and grew strong, while perceptions of the war that was raging in Spain reinforced British

Conservative hostility to Soviet Russia and precluded rapprochement with it. Into this vacuum stepped Hitler. The ensuing Nazi–Soviet Pact sealed Poland's fate, and British and French intervention against the Third Reich on 3 September 1939.

Questions

1. What might be said in favour of the non-intervention policy?
2. 'In reality, neither Britain nor France had any intention of adhering to the non-intervention policy themselves, let alone enforcing it upon others.' Discuss.

SOURCES

1. GUERNICA

Source A: from G.L. Steer's report published in *The Times* and *New York Times*, 28 April 1937.

Monday was the customary market day in Guernica ... At 4.30 p.m., when the market was full and peasants were still coming in, the church bell rang the alarm for approaching aeroplanes, and the population sought refuge in cellars and in the dugouts prepared following the bombing of the civilian population of Durango on March 31, which opened General Mola's offensive in the north ...

In a street leading downhill from the Casa de Juntas [next to the Sacred Tree and where the Basque parliament sometimes sat] I saw a place where 50 people, nearly all women and children, are said to have been trapped in an air raid refuge under a mass of burning wreckage. Many were killed in the fields, and altogether the deaths may run into hundreds. An elderly priest named Aronategui was killed by a bomb while rescuing children from a burning house.

The tactics of the bombers ... were logical: first, hand grenades and heavy bombs to stampede the population, then machine-gunning to drive them below, next heavy and incendiary bombs to wreck the houses and burn them on top of their victims.

The only counter-measures the Basques could employ, for they do not possess sufficient aeroplanes to face the insurgent fleet, were those provided by the heroism of the Basque clergy ...

Source B: the Conservative MP Sir Arnold Wilson rebuts the testimony of G.L. Steer.

The news of the destruction of Guernica, and the statement that it was the direct result of an air attack on a market day, was contained in a telegram to *The*

Times from its special correspondent, Mr G.L. Steer. The wording suggested that he had been an eye-witness of the events he described. Subsequent messages made it clear that he had not, in fact, been within many miles of Guernica at the time of its destruction, and that he had relied for his vivid narrative upon the panic-stricken reports of refugees. He did not, on his own showing, reach Guernica till 2 a.m. on April 27th, some six or six and a half hours after the alleged bombardment had ceased, and even then he was not allowed in the centre of the town. Having claimed that it had been destroyed by air, Mr Steer stuck to his story, and has since published a book in which without adducing any new evidence, he repeats his version of events.[21]

Source C: from *Searchlight on Spain* by Katharine Atholl, 1938.

The effect of this holocaust on public opinion all the world over was so tremendous that . . . attempts were made by the insurgent authorities to disclaim responsibility . . .

[Three] British journalists, Mr Steer, Reuters' correspondent, and Mr Noel Monks of the *Daily Express*, have described how they were all machine-gunned together from 'planes that afternoon, some miles from Gernika, and how they saw 'planes in the direction of Gernika and heard the sound of bombing. Mr Gerahty, the *Daily Mail* correspondent with the insurgents, also from Vitoria saw their bombers flying into the Basque country on the 26th . . . There is no question, therefore, that insurgent 'planes were 'up' and over or near Gernika on the day of its destruction.

It has since been suggested on behalf of the insurgents that, though a few bombs may have been dropped on the town, the fires which finally destroyed it were caused by Basque or [Asturian] incendiaries. But the testimony of many people questioned in Gernika that night . . . was unanimous as to the causes of the tragedy, and the *Star* correspondent, who was actually watching the bombardment from 5 p.m. states that German 'planes 'dropped a succession of incendiary and high-explosive bombs for three hours'.

Source D: from Father Alberto Onaindía's eyewitness report.

The aeroplanes came low, flying at two hundred metres. As soon as we could leave our shelter, we ran into the woods, hoping to put a safe distance between us and the enemy. But the airmen saw us and went after us . . . The *milicianos* and I followed the flight patterns of the aeroplanes and we made a crazy journey through the trees, trying to avoid them. Meanwhile women, children and old men were falling in heaps, like flies, and everywhere we saw lakes of blood.

I saw an old peasant standing alone in a field: a machine-gun bullet killed him. For more than an hour these eighteen planes, never more than a few hundred metres in altitude, dropped bomb after bomb on Guernica. The sound of the explosions and of the crumbling houses cannot be imagined ... Bombs fell by thousands. Later we saw the bomb craters. Some were sixteen metres in diameter and eight metres deep.

The aeroplanes left around seven o'clock, and then there came another wave of them, this time flying at an immense altitude. They were dropping incendiary bombs on our martyred city. The new bombardment lasted thirty-five minutes, sufficient to transform the town into an enormous furnace ... I realized the terrible purpose of this new act of vandalism. They were dropping incendiary bombs to try to convince the world that the Basques had fired their own city.

The destruction of Guernica went on altogether for two hours and forty-five minutes. When the bombing was over, the people left their shelters. I saw no one crying. Stupor was written on all their faces. Eyes fixed on Guernica, we were completely incapable of believing what we saw.

Source E: 'Juana Sangroniz', the pseudonym of a Carlist living in Guernica, interviewed by Ronald Fraser in the 1970s.

Our consciences were uneasy about it. After living through the raid, we knew only too well that the destruction had come from the air. The reds had hardly any planes, we knew that too. Amongst our own we'd admit the truth: our side had bombed the town and it was a bad thing. 'But what can we do about it now?' we'd say; it was better simply to keep quiet. The propaganda was so patently untrue.[22]

Questions

1. Identify (a) General Mola (Source A); (b) *milicianos* (Source D). (2)
2. How far does Source C corroborate Source A, and why would Sir Arnold Wilson (Source B) seek to question their version of events? (6)
3. What are the strengths of Sources A and D as evidence and how does Source D influence the credibility of Source A? (6)
4. What is the particular value of Source E to the historian of Spain during and after the Civil War? (3)
*5. Using your own knowledge and these sources, discuss the reasons why Guernica is regarded as 'the worst atrocity of the Spanish Civil War'. (8)

Worked answer

*5. [Be as precise and as wide-ranging as you can, giving balanced coverage to the 'own knowledge' and 'these sources' aspects. You will

need to place Guernica in the wider Spanish Civil War context for an
effective answer.]

The bombing of Guernica, lying to the north-east of Bilbao and twenty
kilometres from the military front, was the first destruction by carpet
bombing of an undefended civilian town. Being the ancient capital of the
Basque Country, Guernica was rooted deep in the Basque psyche.
Source A refers to the parliament building (Casa de Juntas), home of
Basque democracy. At the nearby Sacred Tree, Spanish monarchs swore
to respect Basque laws.

On market day, 26 April 1937, over fifty German and Italian aircraft,
at the bidding of Franco's High Command, carried out a deliberate act
of terror designed to break Basque morale at this historic point of their
identity. Source A describes a brutally logical scheme of attack with
which to cause maximum death and destruction; the *Star* correspondent
cited in Source C saw three hours of high-explosive and incendiary
bombing, low and high level respectively, according to the eyewitness
in Source D. Three thousand incendiaries fell on Guernica, Source D
adding that they were used so that the Nationalists could pretend arson
by the town's inhabitants. By their onslaught on Guernica, the Condor
Legion could, without risk of counter-attack, perfect the use of new
combat aircraft. George Steer (Source A), who arrived soon after the
bombing and so could not give a conclusive figure, said deaths 'may well
run into hundreds', and he noted the large number of non-combatants
killed; Source D also refers to the machine-gunning of defenceless
civilians and to incredulous survivors of the raid. Altogether there were
perhaps 1,600 deaths and 900 wounded, one-third of the town's
population. Sir Arnold Wilson in Source B is contemptuous of the
evidence of 'panic-stricken refugees', but why should their evidence be
ipso facto unreliable? Source E, in contrast, accepts guilt. 'Hardly any
planes' suggests that the town was defenceless, while demolishing the
feasibility of a deliberately self-inflicted Republican attack. In 1997 the
Basques received an official apology from the German state for 'the most
terrible atrocities' committed by German aircraft against their spiritual
capital. Source C describes Guernica as a 'holocaust' with a 'tremendous
effect' on world opinion. Devout Catholic Basques had been murdered
in the name of self-professed defenders of the Roman Catholic Church.
Many churchmen, Catholic and Protestant, condemned the atrocity, and
for weeks there were high-profile reports in the international press. The
subsequent evacuation of 13,000 Basque children, along with Picasso's
painting of the Guernica outrage, contributed much to the heightened
awareness of this war without pity. Picasso's monochrome masterpiece,

unveiled in July 1937 at the Paris World Fair, since reproduced in countless publications and prominently exhibited, first in New York and now Madrid, has become a defining reference point for posterity.

Abductions by killer squads and the murder of 6,800 clergy notwithstanding, there was no comparable equivalent of Guernica inflicted by the Republic. In terms of numbers killed, there were worse atrocities committed by the Nationalists and their fascist associates. Seville in July 1936, for example, witnessed the slaughter by Nationalist troops of as many as 9,000 workers; in March 1938 Italian bombing raids on Barcelona accounted for 3,000 deaths. Guernica, however, tapped a particular vein of outrage, as a massacre of the innocents in unparalleled circumstances. In the bleakest terms of human tragedy, and made indelible by the power of art, the unique place of Guernica in the collective memory is assured.

SOURCES

2. LEFT-WING VOLUNTEERS IN SPAIN

Source F: from *A Moment of War* by Laurie Lee, 1991.

'Comrades!' he cried. 'It is a special honour for me to stand before you at last – heroic defenders of democracy, champion fighters against the Fascist hordes ... '
It was Harry Pollitt, leader of the British Communist Party ...

He was my first experience of a professional working-class leader ... Wilting though we were, he had us convinced that not only would we smash Franco, Hitler and Mussolini, but go on to capture the whole world for the workers. We were all heroes, and he was our leader, and we cheered him as he stood there, larger than life, shining noble and shaking with emotion.

Then it was all over. The spell and the magic quite broken. He jumped down from the platform to mix with the men and was immediately surrounded by a jostling crowd ... plucking at his sleeves and pouring out their grievances, asking to be sent back home. 'It ain't good enough, you know. I bin out 'ere over nine months. Applied for leave and didn't get no answer. When they goin' to do something, eh, comrade? ... eh? ... ' The last I saw of [him], he was backing towards the door ... eyes groping for escape: 'Sorry, lads – sorry ... nowt to do with me ... sorry, I can't do owt about that ... '

Source G: from *The Owl of Minerva* by Gustav Regler, 1959.

A strong magnetic power emanated from Madrid and those voluntary units. They have called us adventurers and ascribed to us a considerable number of crimes.

Koestler in his obituary of Orwell talks about the 'sham-fraternity' of the International Brigade. But how could a troop exist and win the most difficult battles if their main duty were that of field-gendarmes, their ambition plunder and their morale a sham-fraternity? . . .

'I've come out of Dachau,' said Hans Beimler, the Bavarian leader of the Germans. He had got away to Prague and then had become a member of the Central Committee of the exiled German Communist Party . . . 'The only way we can get back to Germany is through Madrid,' Beimler said.

Source H: from *For Whom the Bell Tolls* by Ernest Hemingway, 1940.

Gomez saw his face clearly in the light and recognized him. He had seen him at political meetings and he had often read articles by him in *Mundo Obrero* translated from the French. He . . . knew him for one of France's great modern revolutionary figures who had led the mutiny of the French Navy in the Black Sea. Gomez knew this man would know where Golz's headquarters were and be able to direct him there. He did not know what this man had become with time, disappointment, bitterness both domestic and political, and thwarted ambition . . . He stepped forward into the path of this man, saluted with his clenched fist and said, 'Comrade Massart, we are the bearers of a dispatch for General Golz. Can you direct us to his headquarters? It is urgent' . . .

'You have what, Comrade?' he asked Gomez, speaking Spanish with a strong Catalan accent. His eyes glanced sideways at Andrés, slid over him, and went back to Gomez.

'A dispatch for General Golz to be delivered at his headquarters, Comrade Massart' . . .

'Where is it from, Comrade?'

'From behind the fascist lines,' Gomez said.

André Massart extended his hand for the dispatch and the other papers. He glanced at them and put them in his pocket.

'Arrest them both,' he said to the corporal of the guard. 'Have them searched and bring them to me when I send for them.'

Source I: from *Volunteers in Spain: Twelve Sublime Months!* by André Marty, 1937.

A political section with its own Press services, *communiqués*, literature in twelve languages and its system of political soldier-militants . . . From the Casa del Campo (Madrid) to Andujar (Cordoba), from Guadalajara to Belchite, from Almeria to the Jarama River, there was not a single battle in which the Internationals did not take part . . . The Spanish Republic would long ago have been crushed but for the creation of a great popular army directed by a sole command. The

International Brigades have been one of the bases for this new army, thanks to their high technical qualifications and strong discipline . . .

The Communists can be proud . . . In the course of twelve months they have been the worthy members of this workers' revolutionary party of a new type, the Bolshevik world party . . . they are now the worthy children of that party which, formed and directed by the greatest brains of to-day, Lenin and Stalin, has upset the whole world. Yes, all are worthy of the great George Dimitrov . . . Every international volunteer is a centre of organization and unity; he is more precious than ever . . . They have accomplished their duty . . . North Americans, Canadians, Africans, French . . . all of them are here.

Questions

1. Explain the references to (a) Dachau (Source G); (b) Dimitrov (Source I). (2)
2. What can be inferred from Source F of the motives and morale of Lee and his comrades, and how far does Source G contradict these inferences? (7)
*3. How authoritative do you find Source H as an evocation of Spain through the eyes of an American? (4)
4. What issues are raised by the origins and content of Source I? (4)
5. Using all these sources and your own knowledge, what conclusions can be drawn about the experiences of left-wing volunteers in Spain? (8)

Worked answer

*3. [Be aware of Hemingway's synthesis of fact and fiction. Also note the role of personal experience in influencing the authority with which he evokes Spain at war.]

The noted author Ernest Hemingway began *For Whom the Bell Tolls* in the closing weeks of the Spanish Civil War, writing with a subtly individual perspective on the conflict. Although *For Whom the Bell Tolls* is fiction, it is based on fact. It avoids crude pro-Republican propaganda; nor does it reflect official Washington policy, which remained isolationist and sceptical of the democratic claims of the Republic. Though the book presents a microcosm of the wider Spanish conflict, it is set during the Segovia Campaign of May 1937. In command of three brigades was a Polish General, Walter, whom Hemingway knew well and who in the novel becomes 'General Golz' (Source H). Other leading characters in *For Whom the Bell Tolls* are also based on fact, including

Source H's 'André Massart', in real life the Comintern's André Marty. The references to his career, speech, appearance and character can be corroborated. Historians Paul Preston and Tom Buchanan describe Marty, respectively, as 'brutal' and 'volatile', while, to Jason Gurney, Marty appeared 'demented'. But another side of Marty is revealed in Source I.

In *For Whom the Bell Tolls* Hemingway writes not altogether sympathetically about the Spanish Republic at war, as Source H demonstrates. By exposing the betrayals that undermined the Republic from within, Hemingway avoids the distortions of propaganda. Although with such a novel dramatic licence is to be expected, *For Whom the Bell Tolls* conveys a 'tough-minded sense of the actual' (Carlos Baker). A bridge between fact and fiction, this classic drama is a conduit to the Civil War experience and is a revealing primary source in its own right.

6

POLITICS ON THE REPUBLICAN SIDE AND THE ROLE OF THE SOVIET UNION

BACKGROUND NARRATIVE

From the start of the military insurrection until Franco's declaration that the Civil War had ended, the governments of Republican Spain were led by five Popular Front premiers: Casares Quiroga (mid-May–18 July 1936), Martínez Barrio (18–19 July 1936), Giral (19 July–4 September 1936), Largo Caballero (4 September 1936–15 May 1937) and Negrín (15 May 1937–finally departed Spain 7 March 1939).

During the Giral period, political power became decentralized and radicalized. Where the Nationalist coup failed, the opportunity was grasped to establish revolutionary committees. In Barcelona, an Anti-Fascist Militias Committee representing a broad section of left-wing groups had the greater share in a 'dual power' with the Generalitat. In Aragón, an autonomous Defence Council, led by the CNT, was set up to coordinate the extensive collectivization in that region. This localism led to what Hugh Thomas has called an 'agglomeration of republics' and it was, ironically, a key feature in the revolution that Franco and Mola had risen up to prevent.[1] So was collectivization, of not only land and factories, but consumer enterprises, including cinemas and restaurants. The upheaval in industry and banking was not as widespread in Madrid, but even here a *de facto* authority was wielded by the UGT, CNT and PCE.

This period of idealism and local democracy had its grim counter-point, however, in an orgy of blood by anarchist 'uncontrollables'. To establish an orderly legal system for punishing 'enemies of the new Spain', Popular Front tribunals came into force by the end of August 1936. Military indiscipline had already contributed to failure at the Guadarrama Passes north of Madrid and in Aragón, where the Durruti Column had failed to recapture Zaragoza. The message that discipline was integral to military success was being preached by the new 'Fifth Regiment', which had attached to it Soviet-style political commissars.

The Soviet connection with the Republic was significantly extended in August: Russian oil shipments began to arrive, together with the Soviet Ambassador Marcel Rosenberg and Senior Military Counsellor General Berzin. In September Alexander Orlov arrived, with orders to construct an NKVD apparatus to combat elements such as the POUM, which was accused of Trotskyism by its Stalinist enemies. As already suggested, however, this sense of a 'new order' was not only expressed externally. In early September Largo Caballero formed the first true Popular Front government with the PSOE, PCE, Left Republicans and PNV (Basque Nationalist Party). Largo, who had until recently refused to be in government, was now determined to take the political initiative after the spontaneous and somewhat debilitating period of revolution. War must be waged rather than improvised. That the USSR and the Comintern would be part of this process was to make for an uneasy liaison. However, thanks partly to Soviet advice, Republican forces were reorganized into a People's Army with 'mixed brigades'. The International Brigades, coordinated by the Comintern, at last arrived in mid-October along with Soviet arms shipments. The IBs would in the next twelve months fight fascism in the raw – in the battles for Madrid, the Jarama River, Guadalajara, Brunete and in Aragón.

In Barcelona in September 1936 the Generalitat, in a move to the right, dissolved the Anti-Fascist Militias Committee. It also limited collectivization to concerns with more than 100 workers: thus small private enterprises would also prosper. Although the prestige of Largo Caballero's central government was undermined when, on

6 November, it hurriedly relocated from Madrid to Valencia, the new Madrid 'Defence Junta' coordinated the capital's resistance against the impending Nationalist attack, with the PCE holding the pivotal public order, militia and supplies portfolios. (By the end of 1936 there had been thirty-three arms deliveries from the USSR, thus grafting more influence on to the PCE's already proven organizational skills.)

How embracing and durable would the Popular Front prove to be? Conflict on the Republican side reflected a significant contrast. Largo Caballero dissolved the Madrid 'Defence Junta' in April 1937 because of what he saw as excessive Stalinist influence. In Barcelona, however, it was the *anti*-Stalinist groupings, most prominently the POUM, that were purged. Carr has described the 'May Days' and their aftermath as 'the watershed in the political life of the Republic' and Esenwein and Shubert hailed them '[as marking] the beginning of communist hegemony in the republican camp' – though by mid-1937 the USSR's interest in the Republic's future was beginning to fade.[2] Having refused to outlaw the POUM, and isolated from his hard-line colleagues, Largo Caballero resigned in May 1937. The government of his successor, fellow-Socialist Negrín, banned the POUM, dissolved the Defence Council of Aragón, and set an agenda for national economic planning. Again, central authority must be recaptured if the war was to be won, and a liberal democratic system confidently sustained in peace.

But could the war be won? Negrín's minister of national defence, Prieto, was not at all convinced that it could, and had made peace overtures to the Nationalists. Negrín accepted his resignation in early April 1938 and himself took over Prieto's portfolio. Now the Aragón front collapsed and the forces of Falangist General Yagüe reached the sea, cutting the Republic in two. Negrín's own subsequent 'Thirteen Points' failed to convince Franco to end the war. Added to this, the Republicans' Ebro Valley Offensive, which began impressively in July 1938, proved a triple disaster – in lives, *matériel* and morale. Political confidence was shaken to its roots by the Munich Agreement in September: if Chamberlain and Daladier would work with Hitler against Czechoslovakia, why should they work against him in Spain?

Now the Republic collapsed. In December Franco mounted his offensive against Catalonia which fell in early February 1939: the last instalment of Soviet aid had failed to arrive in time. Britain and France then ended Republican hopes by recognizing Franco as head of the Spanish state. In early March a new 'civil war within the civil war' erupted when the Republican Colonel Casado, determined to sue for peace with the Nationalists, launched a military–civilian coup against Negrín, the PCE and what little remained of the Soviet presence. But General Franco would not accept the terms put forward by Casado's National Defence Council: they had to accept Franco's. So ended the Spanish Civil War. Albacete, site of the International Brigades' Comintern HQ, and Cartagena, where the first Soviet arms had landed in October 1936, were among the last towns to be occupied by the Nationalists.

ANALYSIS (1): HOW DID THE INTERNATIONAL BRIGADES AND THE USSR AFFECT THE COURSE AND OUTCOME OF THE WAR?

As has been seen in earlier chapters, the crash of revolution against reaction in the summer of 1936 resonated far beyond Spain. In the process, it produced responses that ranged from the altruistic to the Machiavellian. In the context of the Spanish Civil War, the concept of 'foreign volunteer' embraced a wide variety of beliefs and goals. This discussion will focus on the role of the International Brigades and the USSR, and contrasting views of their impact on the Spanish conflict.

The connections between the International Brigades and the USSR are open to interpretation. Was it with the approval of the Soviet government that the Comintern recruited the IBs (Alpert) or did Moscow request the Comintern to do it (Smyth)?[3] Whatever its origins, the process of IB recruitment was organized by national Communist Parties and Comintern agents. That there were no Soviet names attached to these brigades is not surprising, since the Comintern 'line' was that this was an anti-fascist war for Spanish democracy, not a revolutionary war waged by the working class against capitalism. In this way the democracies abroad might be actively engaged in the Republican cause. On the other hand, the Comintern also ensured that Communists played a pivotal role in the IBs, not least as political commissars.

Contemporary perceptions of the International Brigades varied widely. Franco himself referred to the decisive part played by 'foreign, perfectly organized units' in the Nationalists' failure to capture Madrid in 1936–7. In contrast, International Brigader Jason Gurney was deeply critical of IB organization and described André Marty, the French Comintern supremo at Albacete, as 'quite literally mad at this time'.[4] Soon disillusioned by his experiences, Gurney came to see himself as a pawn in a propaganda game. But for Gurney and his fellow-idealists, the Spanish Civil War *per se* was a prophetic metaphor for their own national liberation, an episode in a long and continuing crusade against the right's abuse of power. Black Sea and Invergordon mutineers, victims of racism and the dole, leftists persecuted by fascist regimes, free-speech campaigners, pro-Bolshevik veterans of the Russian Civil War and intellectuals of all classes nailed their colours to the mast and would in later conflicts affirm the same spirit of commitment, despite the hostility of their national governments. The 35,000-plus IB volunteers in Spain operated within the Republican People's Army and were, from 1937, formally integrated into it. They comprised 15 per cent of the forces defending Madrid in late 1936 and 18 per cent of the Republican army brigades at Brunete in July 1937.

Since Franz Borkenau's sweeping assertion in the spring of 1937 that, 'In fact, not Miaja but Kléber [Commander of the Eleventh IB], not the Spanish militia but the international brigades, had saved and still continued to save Madrid',[5] historians have evaluated and re-evaluated the IBs' role in that military sector. Writing in the mid-1970s, Gabriel Jackson highlighted the IBs' example to the militias in not wasting ammunition and in defensive tactics. For Stanley Payne, however, their role was secondary: Madrid's defence was mainly achieved by the leftist militias.[6] For Hills, although the IBs helped delay the Nationalists' advance and crossing of the River Manzanares, their role in the capital's defence was 'important but not decisive'. Though Thomas affirms that the IBs limited the Nationalist advance in the University City, he and Mitchell concur that the Nationalists' momentum had already been checked before the IBs arrived. More recently, Preston has re-emphasized the Eleventh Brigade's vital defensive role and the Internationals' importance in weapons training and morale-building.[7] Whatever qualifications may be made, it is undeniable that a role in the saving of Madrid can be ascribed to the IBs.

The International Brigades, Borkenau had written, 'continued to save Madrid'. The defence of Republican territory in the Battles of the Jarama and Guadalajara formed part of this process. In *Crusade in Spain*, written in the early 1970s, Jason Gurney threw a searchlight on to the IBs' experience at Jarama: comradeship, heroism and individual cases of inspired leadership set against incompetence, squalor and tragedy. But despite appalling losses on the Republican side, including the British and American battalions of the IBs, the Nationalists failed to cut communications between Madrid and Valencia. Nor, at the Battle of

Guadalajara in the following month, did they succeed in their advance on Madrid from the east. Borkenau went so far as to describe the Eleventh and Twelfth IBs as 'the best brigades in the whole Spanish army'.[8] But the humiliating success of the Garibaldi Battalion's Italian exiles against the CTV may well have reinforced Mussolini's resolve to hold out for a Franco victory by any means possible. Whatever the case, the CTV were to have their revenge against the IBs in Aragón, while, more immediately, the Nationalists' failure at Guadalajara was to spell a grim future for the Republican north − soon to be the focus of Mola's wrath by land, sea and air.

Of the Battle of Brunete (July 1937), Hills asserts, 'This battle, unlike Brihuega [part of the Battle of Guadalajara] was overwhelmingly between Spaniards; especially at the most important and basic level of all, the infantry private.'[9] Indeed, though all five IBs took part (Eleventh to Fifteenth), there were also twenty-three Spanish brigades in the field. Yet Brunete was in some senses the IBs' battle. They established a key bridgehead east of the Guadarrama River, and the British Battalion was in the thick of the desperate fighting, at the end of which only 7 per cent of its force of 600 were still battleworthy. Amid bitter recriminations, the British Battalion leaders were summoned to Communist Party HQ in London, while the Thirteenth IB mutinied and was eventually dissolved. Nevertheless, thanks to Brunete, Franco's offensive in the north was disrupted.

A description of the Republican success in capturing Teruel (late December 1937) as 'a bloody victory for an objective of little significance'[10] can be challenged. The logic of Republican strategy could not be faulted − to pre-empt a Nationalist attack, ease communications with Aragón, and obstruct Nationalist routes out of Zaragoza. Similar rationality underpinned the Ebro Valley Offensive, launched by the Republic in July 1938 and the IBs' last great confrontation with fascism in Spain: namely, to reconnect Catalonia with Spain's central heartland and deflect the Nationalists from Valencia. But in both campaigns the Nationalists ultimately prevailed. Having suffered terrible losses in its attempt to take Hill 481, the British Battalion was finally withdrawn from the Ebro Campaign, and the war, in late September 1938, along with the nearly 13,000 other foreign volunteers operating in IB units. Neither the Condor Legion nor the CTV would follow their example.

The left-wing French historians Broué and Témime wrote in 1961, 'Whatever their political views, journalists and writers have always stressed the influence of the commitment of the International Brigades in the stiffening of Republican resistance. They formed a corps d'elite involved in all the fighting of any importance until the end of October

1938.'[11] Enrique Líster suggested in the early 1980s that the IBs were 'ambassadors representing millions of people in the world who were on the side of the Republic, on the side of Spanish democracy. Additionally, they played an important part in this or that battle.'[12]

The Spanish Civil War became a phenomenon of history in which the International Brigades stand out in sharp relief. If Britain, France and the United States were not persuaded that Spanish democracy was a cause to which their own armies or armaments should be committed, who else was there apart from the brigaders to assist the Republic? Moreover, the IBs played a prominent role in defining the images we have of the Spanish Civil War, in written, oral and visual form. The names of their battalions and companies – Thaelmann, Garibaldi, Louis Michel, Lincoln, Dombrowski and Attlee – are testimony to the historical and moral imperative they embraced then and continue to personify now.

Buchanan has pointed out that it was the international communist movement that made the IBs possible. The Third Communist International, or Comintern, had been established in Moscow in 1919 to promote international revolution. However, it adopted a Popular Front policy in 1935 – an anti-revolutionary stance that was consistent with Stalin's Socialism in One Country doctrine and appropriate to Spain's need for a broad pro-democracy front against fascism. Apart from organizing the International Brigades, the Comintern had already inspired the Fifth Regiment (which Líster described as 'a powerful preparation for the communist approach to the war'), which in turn invoked a new professionalism in the Republican army.[13] Comintern officials such as Marty and Togliatti sat in on PCE executive meetings just as Soviet generals participated in those of the General Staff. The PCE and PSUC were Comintern affiliates; both welcomed a wide range of potential members.

The American Cold War historian and diplomat George F. Kennan wrote in 1960, 'Eventually the Comintern gained strength and came to command the loyalty, and even obedience, of a sizable left-wing minority among the European labour movement. It remained, however, under strictest domination of the Russian communists, and soon became . . . a vehicle for the policies of the Soviet leaders rather than a political instrument and mouthpiece of international communist sentiment.'[14] But in the context of Spain, Kennan's apparent inference that its 'policies' were motivated by Soviet imperialism is wide of the mark. For Soviet intervention was primarily, at least in the short and medium term, defensive; as Denis Smyth has pointed out, it was intended to encourage British and French intervention in Spain to defend the Republic and also their partnership with the Soviet Union in an anti-fascist European bloc.

Whatever British and French perceptions were, the USSR intervened in Spain with vitally timed *matériel* and military advisers who, monitored by Orlov's NKVD, were attached to the staffs of Republican generals and played a significant part in the field, for example, at Guadalajara. Russians helped to implement the Republican war in the air, and, on the ground, to train the mixed brigades; Líster and Kléber had attended military training school in Moscow. The *quid pro quo* for such assistance was a political, economic and diplomatic presence in Spain, 'constructive' or 'insidious' depending on the perspective adopted; indeed, gratitude for Soviet food and state-of-the-art aircraft was paralleled by resentment of 'Russian police methods [which], like Russian propaganda, were crude and offended patriotic susceptibilities'.[15]

At government level, both Largo Caballero and Prieto had complicated relations with the USSR and PCE. But the line of argument advanced by historian Burnett Bolloten to the effect that Largo's successor Negrín (Prime Minister May 1937–March 1939) was a puppet both of an imperialistic Stalin and a power-hungry Stalinist PCE has been disputed. Such writers as Angel Viñas in Spain and Helen Graham in the UK are concerned to place Negrín and the PCE in a more three-dimensional context: thus, the PCE was a coherent force in consolidating the Republican war machine, just as Negrín's government needed all the Soviet aid Stalin could be persuaded to give, especially after the grave setbacks of 1938, whatever the price.[16] Negrín also hoped that aid could so prolong the war that Britain and France would intervene when the conflict in Spain fused with the anticipated mass assault by European (including Spanish) fascism. But Colonel Casado believed Negrín's reliance on the PCE was endangering the hope of a negotiated settlement with Franco. Hence his coup against Negrín and the 'resisters' in March 1939.

In the final analysis, the impact of the USSR can be perceived on at least four levels: that of an 'alien' ideology that engendered Franco's crusade; that of direct intervention, crucial to the Republic's survival; through the Comintern and the International Brigades; and through the PCE and PSUC with whom the USSR had close contact. The gradual withdrawal from the Republic of direct Soviet support was one of several factors subverting the Republic's ability to wage war effectively.

After the end of the war, Franco remained committed to his long-standing anti-communist crusade. In Spain he had defeated an enemy but not a doctrine; abroad he would assist Hitler in his equally obsessive project. But in the latter case neither the Soviet army nor Soviet ideology would succumb to the Caudillo's and the Führer's zeal.

Questions

1. In what respects did the International Brigades play a controversial role in the Spanish Civil War?
2. What were the limitations of Russian aid to the Spanish Republic?

ANALYSIS(2): HOW UNITED WERE THE REPUBLICANS?

In this analysis 'Republicans' will be taken to mean 'loyalists' or 'anti-Nationalists'. However, we may preface this question with another: how united was the Popular Front before the Civil War? That divisions predated the upheavals of July 1936 is evident from the fact that the Popular Front alliance party winning the most seats in the February 1936 elections, the PSOE, stood outside the government for seven months, and that internally, since 1934 at least, the PSOE had been in an increasingly fractious state. Concerning the war itself, it would be wrong to opt for stereotypes and sweeping assumptions to the effect that 'Spain was hopelessly divided'. After all, the political situation on the Republican side was extremely fluid and alignments were made as often as they were broken.

It can be postulated that the Republic faced a common enemy and was united by the experience of war. But was 'the enemy' uniquely synonymous with 'Nationalist', and did the experience of war divide the Republic as much as it bound it together? Was 'unity' seen as relevant by all on the Republican side; was it even acceptable, for example, to rank-and-file anarchists if it meant alliance with the 'regimented centralism' of the PCE? Admittedly, to some extent Republican unity rested on tolerance of regional differences and apparently incompatible political identities. Paradoxically, a division of minds was integral to 'Republican identity'. Indeed, historians such as Malefakis, Carr, and Esenwein and Shubert have drawn attention to contrasting 'models' of Republican Spain and what these models – the conventional and the revolutionary; the centralist and the separatist – say about conceptions of how to win the war.[17]

Franco's military successes bit deeply into the geographical unity of the Republic, although this unity was always qualified by differences in regional consciousness and governing institutions. The Basque Country, for example, was both more pluralistic and more conservative than other Republican regions. A glance at a map of the respective 'zones' soon after the outbreak of war shows much of the far north cordoned by insurgent territory from the rest of the Republic. The

Basques' Autonomy Statute of October 1936 nominally secured their commitment to the Republican cause. However, the Basque armed forces, with their various political battalions and priests instead of commissars, were never fully integrated into the Republican Army of the North, and military cooperation with the Asturians further west, with their 'revolutionary hooliganism',[18] proved controversial. Politically, the Basque Nationalist Party (PNV), led by Basque President Aguirre, dominated the government in Bilbao. But the PNV's harmonious working relationship with the Socialists, Left Republicans, Communists and (more liberal) Basque Nationalist Action Party did not extend to the anarchists, who recoiled at the Basque nationalists' at once 'oppressive' and 'subversive' Catholicism. Evidence that degrees of unity could fluctuate over a period of time is shown by the deteriorating relationship within the Bilbao government between the PNV and the Communists, whose propaganda during the northern military campaigns of 1937 alienated many Basques; and by the unstable connections between the PNV and the central government (whether in Madrid, Valencia, Barcelona or Figueras). For example, the PNV withdrew from the Negrín government in August 1938, angered by its increasing intolerance, and the draconian methods of its security service (the SIM).

The long-standing tensions in Catalonia's relationship with central government have already been discussed. However, the abolition of the Anti-Fascist Militias Committee in September 1936, in an attempt to rationalize the war effort in Catalonia, is relevant here. That committee's representative groups, notably the CNT, PSUC and POUM, were now given responsible office in the Generalitat. The Catalan historian Albert Balcells has described this as a 'new anti-Fascist government of unity'. But this unity was at the CNT's expense, for its rank and file, to whom the concept of 'power' was still anathema, was disgusted. Juan Manuel Molina, CNT Under-Secretary for Defence in the Generalitat, was cursed as a traitor to the anarchist revolution.[19] Furthermore, the POUM's hostile newspaper reports on the Stalinist purges in the USSR risked a backlash from the Republic's one great benefactor. By December 1936 the POUM's own representative in the Generalitat, Councillor for Justice Andreu Nin, had been expelled under PSUC pressure; by June 1937 he was dead at the hands of the NKVD.

Set against, yet inseparable from, this 'division' was another 'unity': the united front against the revolutionary left established by the PSUC in alliance with organizations such as the Catalan Federation of Guilds and Corporations of Small Traders and Manufacturers (GEPCI) and President Companys's Catalan Esquerra Party. This dispute would burst open in the Barcelona 'May Days' of 1937.

The PCE, as the Communist Party of all Spain, also sought a united front of those who, as defined by Raymond Carr, could contribute their skills to the making of victory. Helen Graham also underlines the PCE's flexible appeal to a wide constituency in the middle and working classes. For sceptics at the time, however, '[the PCE's] commonsense policies either concealed a humiliating sacrifice of national policy to Russian pressure or an attempt by a small party to infiltrate the whole machinery of state'.[20]

This same party and Prieto, the PSOE Minister of Defence, had been allies in government under (and, as has been seen, against) the then Prime Minister, Largo Caballero. But the PCE–Prieto alignment was not to last, for Prieto came to see the PCE as a liability, and vice versa. Such were the political tectonics underlying the Popular Front.

Within the Republican army, the greater organizational unity and combat proficiency forged during the first year of the war could not prevent an accumulation of military setbacks and corrosive infighting. However, during the period July 1936–March 1939 the experiences of men and women in Republican Spain reached beyond waging a military war against the Nationalist rebels. Should the significance of developments in Republican Spain be judged solely on the criterion of whether they helped or hindered that war effort? If the answer is no, then a disunity of outlook in the Republican zones can be seen positively – as political, cultural and economic pluralism in action. Moreover, because of the complexity of Spain's history, this diversity was always likely to prevail, though it did not prevent Franco from branding all Republicans as 'reds', united in betrayal of the *Patria*.

Questions

1. During the Civil War period, how significant were regional variations in Republican Spain?
2. 'Republican Spain seemed much more divided than it actually was.' Discuss.

SOURCES

1. JUAN NEGRÍN AND HIS GOVERNMENTS

Source A: Rudolf Rocker, a German anarchist, on Negrín's relations with the UGT, 1937.

[In Catalonia] in that stirring period after the defeat of the Fascist revolt . . . the membership card of a trade-union played an important role and, one might say, served its possessor as a pass.

So it came about that thousands of small managers, tradesmen, local politicians, saloon-owners, government employees, etc., flocked into the UGT unions, which naturally were more to their liking than the old storm-tried organizations of the CNT. And this went on at greater pace as the Communist PSUC, under whose political guardianship the syndicates of the UGT in Catalonia stand, came out more plainly with its attacks on the efforts at socialization of organized labour . . .

Still it is not to be disputed that the UGT is today a serious hindrance to the CNT in Catalonia, and that under the special protection of the Negrin government in Valencia it has grown into a grave danger to all the economic and political achievements of the Spanish working class.

Source B: from Palmiro Togliatti's confidential report to Comintern HQ in Moscow, 30 August 1937.

The . . . overthrow of Largo Caballero's government has undoubtedly gone to the heads of some comrades. They have decided that the success was due solely to the [Communist] party, forgetting that Prieto and the centrists had played a very important role . . . This false assessment contributed to the view coming to the fore that now the party can pose the question of its hegemony, and struggle openly for this hegemony in the government and in the country . . .

In Catalonia . . . the comrades had defined their main task as being to 'struggle for the destruction of all capitalist elements' . . . thus arriving at the logical conclusion that such a policy could be carried out only by a proletarian and communist government . . . It is clear that . . . the confused comrades could not grasp the fact that after the fall of Caballero their task was, on the one hand, to exert pressure on the government to secure the implementation of a popular front policy and, on the other, to prepare an enlargement of the government's basis.

Source C: a critical view of Negrín from Jason Gurney, looking back on his years as an International Brigader.

Largo Caballero, whose premiership had more or less been accepted by all the factions of the Left, had been forced to resign as he would not agree to the destruction of the POUM . . . Negrín, whose very name was totally unknown to the mass of the people, was appointed Prime Minister on the instructions of the Party. He was an intellectual and a man of extreme arrogance . . . and certainly no Communist, but he admired the ruthlessness of the Communist Party policies and thought that he could use them as a tool to centralize the diverse elements in the Republic and bring them into a single planned and efficient unit. It was typical of his arrogance that he believed that he was making use of the Communist Party when, in fact, they were using him. It was agreed between them that the Trades Union movement, both CNT and UGT, were to be united, whether they liked it or not. There was to be no further talk of the Revolution. All political parties were to be strictly subservient to the central Government. We were now fighting solely for the Republic and there must not be any kind of action or propaganda that would upset bourgeois sensibilities. The process of land reform was to be halted and assistance denied to the co-operatives. Everything that the mass of the Republicans thought they were fighting for was cancelled out.

Source D: from *Searchlight on Spain* (1938) by Katharine Atholl.

And the patriotic unity existing on the Republican side is shown by the fact that, in spite of the exclusion of their ministers from the Government, the CNT has lately sent the Prime Minister an assurance of its unconditional support and maximum assistance on behalf of liberty and national independence. On February 10th, 1938, it actually published a programme jointly agreed upon with its great rival, the UGT . . .

The initiative was again taken when in August the Government troops advanced towards Saragossa, capturing Belchite on the way, in spite of hard fighting. The operation was the result of the inclusion of the Catalan forces in the Republican Army. It was evidence of a new unity between Catalonia and the Republic which was one of many results of Señor Negrin's appointment as Prime Minister.

This unity, and the removal of the Republican Government to Barcelona in October, 1937, had another vitally important result . . . Not only munitions, but aeroplanes, began to issue from the Catalan factories in numbers which steadily increased, though they were small compared with the resources available to the insurgents . . .

The reactions to the loss of Teruel reveal the temper of the people. On February 23rd the Ministry of Labour published a decree as a temporary war measure, providing that by March 7th all industries must work a minimum week of forty-eight hours. Some are actually working from fifty-six to sixty-two. Two days later the Union de Muchachas, an organisation of young women, issued a manifesto, urging the Government and labour organisations to enrol women in industry. They ask to take the places left vacant by the men called up by the last mobilisation decree. Nothing could better illustrate the determined spirit in which loyalist Spain is facing tremendous odds . . .

The increased output in the factories has enabled two new classes of men to be called to the colours since the fall of Teruel – those aged 30 and 19 respectively.

Source E: the 'Thirteen Points' – war aims of the Spanish Republic, issued by Negrín's government on 1 May 1938 (summaries appear in italics).

The Government of National Union . . . hereby solemnly declares its war aims to its fellow-countrymen and to the world.

First: To ensure the absolute independence and complete integrity of Spain; a Spain entirely free from all foreign interference . . . with her peninsular and insular territory and her possessions untouched and safe from any attempt at dismemberment, seizure or alienation; and with her protectorate zone, assigned by international agreements, retained . . . Spain will draw more closely together the links forged by a common origin . . . which bind her to the other Spanish-speaking countries.

Second: Withdrawal of foreign military forces.

Third: A people's Republic, represented by a virile state based on the principles of pure democracy . . . with the full authority conferred by universal suffrage . . .

Fourth: No reprisals for anyone participating in a plebiscite on a legal and social structure for the post-war Republic.

Fifth: Without undermining national unity, respect for regional diversity.

Sixth: The Spanish State shall guarantee all citizen rights in civil and social life, liberty of conscience and the free exercise of religious belief and practice.

Seventh: The State shall guarantee legal property . . . It will prevent the exploitation of the citizen and subjugation of collectivity by an accumulation of wealth . . . To this end it will encourage the development of small properties, [and] will guarantee family patrimony . . .

Eighth: Reform of the old system of landownership which lacked 'every human, national and patriotic sentiment'.

Ninth: Rights of workers guaranteed by the State in agreement with the specific necessities of Spanish life and economy.

Tenth: . . . the cultural, physical and moral improvement of the race.

Eleventh: The Spanish army, at the service of the nation itself, shall be free from all hegemony, bias or party, and the people shall recognise it as a sure stronghold for the defence of their liberties and their independence.

Twelfth: ... *The State reaffirms renunciation of war as a tool of national policy, and support for the League of Nations.* Spain, ... claiming as a Mediterranean power her place among the nations, is always ready to collaborate in the support of collective security and the general defence of peace. In order to contribute effectively to this policy, Spain will develop and intensify every possible means of defence ...

Thirteenth: Amnesty for all those involved in reconstruction and restoration of national greatness.

Questions

1. (a) Define 'hegemony' (Sources B and F); (b) What were the main differences between the UGT and the CNT (Sources A and C)? (3)
2. Study Source B. How might its author, Togliatti (an Italian Comintern official in Spain), have responded to Rocker's comments in Source A? (4)
3. How far do Sources C and D provide contrasting inter-pretations of the impact on the Spanish Republic of Negrín's premiership? (5)
*4. Comment on the timing of Source F, and its appeal to a national and international audience. (5)
5. Using these sources and your own knowledge, comment on the view that criticism of Negrín's premiership underestimates its achievements and the pressures with which it was faced. (8)

Worked answer

*4. [Here it is necessary to think about Negrín's motives in publishing this at the beginning of May 1938, the stubborn obstacles he faced, and how quickly the fortunes of war could change.]

The Thirteen Points can be interpreted as a manifesto for a post-war Spanish Republic or, if the chance came, the basis for a negotiated peace with the Nationalists. Already, during April 1938, Prieto had been probing for peace. Indeed, when the Thirteen Points were issued, it seemed as though Negrín might have some negotiating cards up his sleeve: the Republican army in the east had been reorganized, and by the end of April it had ground down the Nationalists' offensive southwards from Teruel;

also, from March the Republic had been receiving new equipment across the French frontier. However, this *matériel* was almost exclusively Russian, and, since Prieto's departure from the Defence Ministry at the beginning of April, Communist influence in Negrín's government had effectively increased. Read in this light, the Thirteen Points can be seen as a cleverly worded counter-offensive against this 'red wedge', an attempt to convince the West that the Republic was not in Moscow's pocket. Source F's moderate tone represented a plea for a broader-based aid programme involving the West. It also hinted at common ground with the Nationalists. Thus the Thirteen Points evoked the spirit of patriotism (e.g. Point 1), the race (Points 1 and 10), and strong government (Point 3). At times, the language and tone echo those of the Nationalists' own Labour Charter.

Only unconditional Republican surrender, however, would satisfy Franco; a compromise peace would not 'finish the reds'. He had no use for a non-political army (Point 11). In any case, Franco could well afford to reject Negrín's proposals, as by May 1938 his ultimate victory was assured.

SOURCES

2. THE USSR: HELP OR HINDRANCE?

Source F: Prime Minister Largo Caballero writes to Stalin, Molotov and Voroshilov, 12 January 1937.

The help you are providing to the Spanish people . . . considering it as your duty . . . has been and continues to be greatly beneficial . . . From the bottom of my heart, and in the name of Spain, and especially on behalf of the workers, we assure you of our gratitude. We trust that . . . your help and advice will continue to be available to us . . .

Those comrades who . . . came to our aid, are rendering us great services. Their vast experience is useful to us and contributes notably to the defence of Spain in her fight against Fascism. I can assure you that they are bringing to their task genuine enthusiasm and extraordinary courage. As to Comrade Rosenberg, I can say in all sincerity that we are satisfied with his behaviour and activity. He is liked by everybody here. He works hard, so hard that this affects his already undermined health.

Source G: Sócrates Gómez of the JSU, interviewed by Ronald Fraser in the 1970s.

The communist party tried to absorb, monopolize everything . . . Instead of unity, there was the opposite. The war was being fought for the freedom of Spain, not to win a victory which would hand the country over to the communists who, in turn, served the interests of another nation. But from the propaganda, the large posters of Stalin, etc., the impression was gained that Spain was in the Soviets' hands. That only alienated large sectors of the population on our side and helped the enemy . . .

To be a socialist where the communist party or JSU was dominant was virtually equivalent to being a criminal. Instead of unity, anyone who protested . . . was slandered, blackened and sometimes physically eliminated. The communist party never attempted to take account, calmly and coolly, of differences of political opinion; they launched instead into insults, slanders, defamations.

Source H: the German anarchist Rudolf Rocker scorns Russian influence in Spain (1937).

In Catalonia, where the Socialists and their trade-union subsidiary, the UGT before the Fascist uprising played no part whatever, the Stalinists, using the catchword of the United Front, succeeded in tricking the Socialist Party and in calling into being the so-called PSUC ('Partido Socialista Unido de Cataluna', United Socialist Party of Catalonia), which soon joined the Third International, and despite its Socialist coat of arms is just an instrument of Moscow. With the arrival of the . . . representatives of Russia this underground boring . . . increased. What the Spanish Stalinists had to learn in this respect was soon taught them by Señors Rosenberg in Madrid and Antonov-Ovsëenko in Barcelona . . . Russian insinuations found willing ears in bourgeois and right Socialist circles and were making themselves heard more and more clearly among the Catalonian Nationalists as well, and deep in the ranks of Caballero's government in Valencia . . .

What the Russian autocrats and their supporters fear most is that the success of libertarian Socialism in Spain might prove to their blind followers that the much vaunted 'necessity of a dictatorship' is nothing but one vast fraud which in Russia has led to the despotism of Stalin.

Source I: Gerald Brenan's evaluation, from *The Spanish Labyrinth* (1943/50)

[The] Russian intervention gave the Communists a position they could never otherwise have held in Spain . . . The prestige of the International Brigade, which had saved Madrid, was another factor. Besides, it seemed that Stalin had been correct in thinking that a moderate Left-wing-line was the one which held the most future for his party. Unable to draw to themselves the manual workers, who remained firmly fixed in their unions, the Communists found themselves the refuge for all those who had suffered from the excesses of the Revolution . . . In Catalonia, where fear and hatred of the Anarchists was very strong, they were able to combine the various Socialist groups . . . into a single party, the PSUC, which was affiliated to the Comintern . . .

But it would be a mistake to suppose that the Communists owed their success merely to their control of Russian arms and to their dislike of social revolution. They had a dynamism that no other party in Government Spain possessed . . . With missionary fervour . . . they set out to conquer the traditional inertia and passivity of the Spanish bureaucratic temperament . . . But it was not easy for other parties to get on with them. They suffered from a fixed belief in their own superior knowledge and capacity. They were incapable of rational discussion. From every pore they exuded a rigid totalitarian spirit . . . To them winning the war meant winning it for the Communist party . . . Thus they kept the Aragon front without arms to spite the Anarchists and prevented a very promising offensive in Extremadura from taking place because the credit for its success might have gone to Caballero.

Source J: from a contemporary analysis by Franz Borkenau (1938).

The trend of Spanish events, then, was diverted by the interference of a Power whose help had been sought on account of its higher technical standards in both military and administrative affairs. As a compensation for help this Power claimed and obtained – besides pay in cash . . . – a decisive influence upon the policy of the Spanish Government . . .

What were the results, in the Government camp? . . . The Russian officers and the non-Russian foreign communist volunteers brought military success; not very splendid success, indeed, but enough to save the republic. The communists . . . obtained the transformation of the old militia into something similar to a modern army . . . The communists, moreover, demanded the creation of a centralized administrative power as against the chaotic rule of local committees; certainly it was a necessity of the war. They objected to the collectivization of the peasants' lots . . . They put a check to wholesale socialization of industry, which was dangerous from more than one point of view. In all these respects, the communists were the executors of the inevitable necessity . . . of concentration of all forces upon the essential aims of the moment . . .

[But] they acted . . . not with the aim of transforming chaotic enthusiasm into disciplined enthusiasm, but with the aim of substituting disciplined military and administrative action for the action of the masses and getting rid of the latter entirely . . .

The old civil service, the old police, certain elements of the old army, large groups of shopkeepers, merchants, well-to-do peasants, intellectuals, begin to take a more active interest in the Government than before, while the poor peasant and the industrial worker are drawing away from it.

Questions

*1. (a) Explain the reference to 'Rosenberg' (Sources F and H);
   (b) Who were the JSU? (Source G)? (3)
2. Why might caution be necessary in considering Source F as evidence of the Republican government's relations with the USSR? (4)
3. To what extent is Source G supported by the arguments in Sources I and J? (6)
4. Illustrate and explain the differences in language and tone of Sources H and I. (4)
5. Referring to these sources and your own knowledge, discuss the view that the USSR had a detrimental effect on the Republican war effort. (8)

Worked answer

*1. [Remember the low tariff here. You will need to write more for part (a) because of 'explain' and 'references'.]

(a) In Source F Largo Caballero could not afford not to praise 'Rosenberg' who, as Soviet Ambassador, was a keystone of aid to the Republic. In Source H, the anarchist Rocker makes a sarcastic reference to Rosenberg as a Spaniard, and implies that he is training the PCE/PSUC to permeate, and thus manipulate, Republican politics and government.

(b) The United Socialist (–Communist) Youth movement.

7

FRANCO AND FASCISM

BACKGROUND NARRATIVE

General Franco's connections with fascism in the later 1930s and 1940s will be explored later. However, that he was already convinced of the benefits of Spanish imperialism and of a centralist, hierarchical Spain inseparable from his own destiny is clear from earlier landmarks in his career. In 1923 he became Commander of the Spanish Legion and, having featured prominently in the humbling of the Moroccan Riffs, was promoted to Brigadier General in 1926. A year later, Miguel Primo de Rivera appointed Franco Commandant of the elite Zaragoza Military Academy. By 1934 a full general, and having masterminded the suppression of the Asturias Revolt, Franco was again promoted: to Commander-in-Chief of Spain's supreme fighting force, the Army of Africa; then, in 1935, to Chief of the General Staff. In this capacity he was to work with José María Gil Robles, CEDA Minister of War and admirer of Nazi propaganda techniques.

Several attempts were made to create fascist mass movements in Spain. Founded in 1931, and yelling, 'Arise! Spain, one, great, free!' the Juntas of the National-Syndicalist Offensive (JONS) modelled themselves on the Nazi Sturmabteilung, and brandished flags of red and black as beacons to the disaffected left. Also embracing the workers within its national 'mandate', the blue-shirted Spanish Phalanx (Falange Española) was born in October 1933. The memory of his father's efforts to forge a 'new politics' was a strong influence on the Falange's charismatic creator, José Antonio Primo de Rivera. He had also learned from the Italian romantic nationalist D'Annunzio and his opportunistic admirer Mussolini, not to mention Sir Oswald Mosley, founder of the British Union of Fascists.

The Falange and JONS merged in March 1934 and in November published a 'Twenty-seven Points' manifesto. Electorally, however, this new Falange Española de las JONS remained weak, polling only 0.7 per cent of the vote in the February 1936 elections and attracting under 3 per cent of right-wing support in Madrid. Even so, despite its official prohibition in March and the jailing of José Antonio, its membership now increased. As the 'revolution' threatened, panic set in on the right: the JAP, youth group of the now-eclipsed CEDA, converted *en masse* to the Falange, whose *escuadristas* (squadristi) stoked the furnaces of looming civil war.

Meanwhile, the new Popular Front government's posting of Franco to the Canaries failed to contain him, and already by late July 1936 the shape of the future Francoist state was being defined. The Law Against Military Rebellion (still in place in the late 1960s) would give legal sanction to the mass execution of 'reds'. The Law of Political Responsibilities (February 1939, vindictively backdated to October 1934) would establish a framework for custody and confiscations. Accompanying a cabinet reshuffle in August 1939, the Law for the Administration of the State was to strengthen Franco's personal grip on the legislative 'process'. In turn, these harsh contours would be extended by the Laws for the Suppression of Freemasonry and Communism (1940) and of State Security (1941).

A celebrated early victim of the Nationalist repression was the internationally acclaimed Granadine poet and playwright, Federico García Lorca. Murdered in August 1936 on the orders of José Valdes, the Falangist Governor of Granada, Lorca had, ironically, been sheltered by Falangist friends. His own martyrdom was followed in November by that of the Falangists' own *jefe nacional*, José Antonio, shot by a Republican firing squad.

Meanwhile, the rebel threat to Madrid had proved serious but not overwhelming. Indeed, it was the Nationalists' failure to seize the capital, along with increasing Soviet aid to the Republic, that helps explain Franco's decision in December 1936 to centralize the Falangist and Carlist militias under army control. But he was also alert to the factions' political aspirations, which he took further steps to neutralize by forming the megalithic 'Falange Española Tradicionalista y de las

JONS' on 19 April 1937. The obliteration of Guernica occurred seven days later. By the end of that year, what had remained of the resources-rich north had fallen to the Nationalists. By the end of 1938, with Republican territory cut in two in the east, Nationalist forces were launching their final offensive in Catalonia. After March 1939 Franco and Francoism remained wedded to violence in their determination to win the 'peace'. More immediately, however, perhaps it was more that the Republic lost the Civil War than that Franco and the Nationalists won it.

ANALYSIS (1): DID THE NATIONALISTS WIN, OR THE REPUBLICANS LOSE, THE SPANISH CIVIL WAR?

This question carries echoes of the Government and Politics 'standard': 'Oppositions do not win elections. Governments lose them.' Discuss. What is inferred is that mistakes on the part of those in power impose the ultimate price: defeat. In the context of the Spanish Civil War, did the Republic, through a catalogue of errors, lose to the Nationalists? Had it, moreover, seized defeat from the jaws of victory? Two hypotheses, admittedly qualified by hindsight, suggest that the Republic might have done just that. Hills, for example, argues that the Republic could have defeated the rebels by August 1936 had it executed a workable masterplan for cordoning Franco in Morocco and Mola in Navarre. Preston suggests that, had the government promptly armed the proletariat, revolt could have been turned into rout. Did a combination of mistakes and misfortune cost the Republic the war? Or were the Nationalists such brilliant tacticians and strategists, with such superior logistics and leadership, that the Republic had no hope of victory?[1]

Payne has written of how Francisco Franco was 'keenly aware of the importance of politicopsychological factors in civil war that made it dangerous not to annul immediately any leftist triumph'.[2] Hence, for example, the relief of the Alcázar, Toledo, in September 1936 and the retaking of Teruel in February 1938 and, by that November, the Republican bridgeheads on the Ebro.

Franco was normally well served by his generals. These included the tireless Dávila, who succeeded Mola in June 1937 as Commander of the Army of the North; Orgaz, efficient overlord of mass conscription from March 1937; and Yagüe, a field commander skilled in rapid movement and the annihilation of resistance, as shown by the Army of Africa's bloody advance from the south in August–October 1936 which brought the Nationalists close to Madrid.

Nationalist air supremacy was gained in 1937, and was decisive in the Northern campaign. On the ground, Franco's speed in deploying reinforcements was put to critical use in July 1937 at Brunete, where the Republic's ultimate failure was to have grave consequences for their position in the north, already jeopardized by the loss of Bilbao. Though the Italian CTV played an important role in this now-renewed Nationalist offensive, the Italian Foreign Minister Ciano was exaggerating matters when, referring to the Catalonian campaign in early 1939, he wrote, '[Our] General Gambara has luckily assumed the role of leader of all Spanish forces.' Nevertheless, German and Italian aid throughout the war was both more abundant and more continuous than that accessible to the Republic. And its timing could be critical, as was the case from October 1938, and Franco's counter-attack on the Ebro and the Catalonia Offensive that followed. Inexorably, the Nationalists strengthened their grip on Spain's domestic resources – human, agricultural, mineral and industrial.

Critically, despite some self-inflicted damage to their moral standing abroad, for instance, Guernica, the Nationalists won the diplomatic war. November 1936 brought recognition by Hitler and Mussolini. Germany and Italy were also represented on the Non-Intervention Committee – which barred its doors to the Spanish Republic. The Nationalists had a sympathetic network in the League of Nations. This buttressed non-intervention and neutralized attempts by the Spanish Republic to make the League confront international aggression against it. In February 1939 came recognition of the Franco regime by Britain and France.

In Spain itself the Nationalists had the high-profile support of the Catholic Church, while the 'old oligarchy' was returned to power and influence, notably in the countryside. However, did Franco believe that he had fully vanquished Marxism, Freemasonry and pluralism by the end of March 1939? If not, when would he be confident enough to terminate the bloody repression of the post-war years? And when this closed regime began to open, could the process ever be reversed?

The Republic, notably in defence, certainly showed prowess during the Civil War: for example, in Madrid during late 1936 and in the hinterland north of Valencia when in the summer of 1938 the Republican Army of the Levante held back the Nationalist advance. General Rojo conceived brilliant plans for offensives during which Republican forces, including the International Brigades, at first struck forward incisively. However, political and military in-fighting often undercut the initial advantage, as at Brunete. At Belchite in Aragón, observes Payne, orders were so detailed as to discourage initiative among field officers,[3] while the Nationalists' recapture of Teruel in February 1938 led to debilitating recrimination within the Republican hierarchy. Whether officers were politically 'sound' was decided by the army's Information and Control Department, which meant that skilled personnel spuriously dubbed 'class enemies' were excised from the war effort. On the other hand, the inadequacy of Republican field officers has been blamed for the loss of Málaga, a working port on the Andalusian coast, in February 1937.

The Republic held numerical advantage at sea but failed to capitalize on it. Many officers had been murdered by their crews in July 1936 and the engineers' and sailors' committees who commandeered the ships did not produce a disciplined strategy for victory at sea. The smaller Nationalist fleet gained naval supremacy and helped deter the transport of much-needed *matériel* to the Republican zone, for example, to Catalonia in early 1939. On the ground, indiscipline contributed to the fall of Málaga and the north ('sudden collapses of weak units which rendered useless the resistance of heroic units'),[4] and to the Nationalists' successful march to the Mediterranean in the spring of 1938, when front-line Republican units disintegrated under the impact of ground and air attack.

If the mobilization of the Republican armed forces was flawed, what of its civilian population? The issue of Republican 'unity' was considered in Chapter 6, but the question can still be posed: Was it enough to be anti-fascist? The script of one anarchist propaganda film described the restaurants of collectivized hotels: 'These large halls which once housed frivolous girls, tycoons, captains of industry, lazy aristocrats and international adventurers are now full of humble men and women living in a new society. Barcelona works and eats. That is its strength and its virtue.' But morale-sapping divisions in Republican Catalonia, along with savage police repression, had long been endured. And by early 1939 Barcelona was starving.[5]

Collectivization of industry and agriculture was and is highly controversial. Carr has argued that, along with the Basques' and Catalans' resolve to protect their autonomy, collectivization 'restricted the creation of a planned economy and hampered the war industry'. Speaking in the early 1980s, José Antonio's sister Pilar Primo de Rivera contrasted what she saw as the 'chaos, the jumble of weird ideas' in the Republican zone with the 'order and tradition' on the Nationalist side. However, she does not mention Negrín's attempts to hammer out a more rational strategy for a war economy.[6]

The Republic had to face many problems, not least the discontinuity in support from the Soviet Union and France. Aid was insufficient to match, let alone prevail over, the Nationalists' strength. It has been said that Negrín's hope was to activate British and French support in a wider war against international fascism. However, the first possible occasion in 1939 when such a war might in theory have broken out was after the Nazis' occupation of Prague on 15 March. Yet fifteen days earlier Britain and France had recognized Franco as *de facto* Head of State.

The Republic lost the war of morale, experiencing a declining faith in victory. However, the Spanish Republic could be said to have won the propaganda war – though this was to prove a pyrrhic victory. Whatever the case, there is a problem in defining who exactly the 'Republicans' were as the war drew to its close in March 1939 – divided as they were between those loyal to Negrín and those determined to bring him down, preferring to 'lose' to Franco rather than to communism. If, however, it is true that the Nationalists 'won' the Spanish Civil War, then Franco soon added vindictiveness to victory – though in the long run democracy would be vindicated over dictatorship.

Questions

1. Why was it Franco rather than Negrín who read out a Victory Proclamation at the end of the Spanish Civil War?
2. Why did it take the Nationalists so long to defeat the Republicans?

ANALYSIS (2): TO WHAT EXTENT WAS FRANCO'S REGIME FASCIST?

In November 1936 Nazi Germany and Fascist Italy accorded Franco diplomatic recognition as Chief of State. By January 1938, when by decree he installed his first government, Franco was firmly established as 'National Chief' of the Falange Española Tradicionalista y de las JONS – the monumental 'movement' that was to underpin his dictatorship. In February 1939 Franco's regime was recognized by Britain and France and, on 1 April and with the Caudillo's deceptive termination of the Civil War, by the United States.

The use of 'fascist' in the title of this analysis conjures immediate associations with Fascist Italy and the Third Reich. However, the founder of the Spanish Falange, José Antonio Primo de Rivera, was at pains to emphasize: 'The movement we have initiated in Spain is not a copy of any foreign movement. It has learned from fascism what fascism has of the idea of unity, authority and the subjugation of the struggles among classes by the idea of cooperation.'[7]

Always aware of the political value of continuity, Franco projected himself as Rivera's* heir, just as in the Soviet Union Stalin had done with Lenin. Moreover, he elevated Rivera in death as the icon of the Nationalist *movimiento*. 'Franco could safely share the leadership of Spain with a dead man who could not contradict the myth imposed on him.'[8]

The Falange would prove a valuable weapon in Franco's hands, and, although its place in his political cosmos was to fluctuate, it would never be totally eclipsed. Many of the Falange's ideas were used, and distorted, by Franco; others were jettisoned. Indeed, revolutionary Falangism was in practice anathema to the Caudillo; thus the banks would not be nationalized, nor would agricultural holdings be redistributed. Instead, the Franco regime repealed the Republic's Agrarian Reform Law and returned collectivized property to its 'original' owners.

In his speech inaugurating the Falange Española in October 1933, Rivera's references to authority and hierarchy implied the centrality of strong leadership. The *teoria de caudillaje* was a defining contour of the Franco regime, and with it came a flourishing personality cult. In the words of the Falangist intellectual Miguel Machado in late 1937, 'the man of providence, chosen by God to carry out the great work, is our unconquered Leader. The man of war and peace. The man of Spain. Franco, Franco, Franco.'[9] Franco embodied, charismatically, the destiny of the Fatherland, a destiny which, as Rivera had argued, would be resolutely protected by rigorous discipline and in a spirit of service and sacrifice. But with the hindsight of the Civil War and particularly the impoverished post-Civil War years, Franco's pledge on his October 1936 investiture that 'Our work requires sacrifices from everyone, principally from those who have more in the interests of those who have nothing' is disingenuous in the extreme.

Order and discipline would promote the cause of a centralist Spain. Rivera had said in November 1934, 'Spain is an indivisible destiny. All separatism is a crime.' Franco was to ban the public use of Galician, Basque and Catalan, and in April 1938 the Autonomy Statutes for the Basque Country and Catalonia were abolished. Ironically, the Galician Franco personified a 'Greater Castilian' chauvinism, just as the Georgian Stalin basked pitilessly in his role as 'Greater Russian' chauvinist.

The Falangist obsession with unity was also reflected in Rivera's call for a corporate state and for the abolition of political parties, the Cortes and the class struggle, of Marxism and its ramifications. Franco himself

* All mentions of Rivera in this chapter refer to José Antonio Primo de Rivera unless otherwise stated.

did not convene a Cortes until 1943. Although no more than a two-thirds-nominated advisory body, for Franco this 'Cortes' was hard political currency. For example, as Sheelagh Ellwood has suggested in her biography, it showed that the political class endorsed 'Franco' legislation such as the 1947 Law of Succession.[10] A subsequent referendum emphasized the point that Franco proceeded by consent. Concerning divisive class conflict, strikes (Rivera's 'anarchy in the workplace') were treason and thus capital offences. Labourers involved in agricultural collectivization were also victimized, and the property of anyone suspected of 'red' tendencies was confiscated. General Queipo de Llano, in Seville, summed up the aim: 'We shall go on to the bitter end and continue our good work until not a single Marxist is left in Spain.'

The Falange, as had others before it, called for national regeneration 'through a fusion of the modern age with the quintessential quality of Spanish nationhood' or *Hispanidad*.[11] Franco certainly sought national regeneration, but he turned his back on modernity. Nevertheless, he shared Rivera's ultra-nationalism and his passion for empire: thus, the Caudillo looked covetously on Gibraltar, Portugal, French North Africa and French Catalonia. Moreover, he embraced the Falangist concept of Spain as 'the spiritual axis of the Spanish-speaking world [which] entitles it to a position of preeminence in world affairs'.[12] Individuals would contribute to national regeneration through the collective task of all Spaniards, namely, work – the right and obligation of all. There would be no 'parasitic citizens'.[13] The concept of *Hispanidad* invoked Spanish distinctiveness and tradition. It thus embraced cultural as well as economic self-sufficiency. 'Death to Culture!' implied death to works considered Marxist, liberal or anti-religious; books which offended against the 'Spanish' spirit were burned in *autos-da-fé*.

Thus, Spain would be 'purified', as it would be by relentless violence against those individuals and groups whose loyalty to the true Spain was suspect. But there were cracks in the consensus concerning the 'dialectic of fists and pistols' that Rivera had believed necessary to combat attempts to 'poison' the Spanish people and to subvert 'justice or the fatherland'. The Franco regime took this brutality to horrific extremes; but, in contrast, Rivera's controversial successor Manuel Hedilla believed in enhancing the working-class 'basis', not destroying it. And the Falangist General Yagüe called in April 1938 for Republican prisoners to be set free, despite his record of repression at Asturias in October 1934. Concerning the Civil War and post-Civil War years, Michael Richards has produced a meticulously documented analysis (ranging from Falangist reports, through communiqués from British diplomats and anecdotal evidence, to contrasting Spanish histories of the period) which underlines the scale of the Francoist repression. Badajoz, Málaga, Seville, Granada, Barcelona – these regions were disciplined like many others by 'Purification Brigades' and bureaucratic 'justice'. As Richards has written, 'Francoist political terror and violence [was] state-directed oppression in the pursuit of a reactionary political project . . . it disoriented Republican strategy and wiped out much of its social support.'[14] Underlining the continuity of war into peace, Preston has concluded that 'Franco's regime would be the institutionalization of his victory in the Spanish Civil War.'[15]

The victorious Francoist state was highly bureaucratic. At this level the Falange played a pervasive role. However, whether they were always 'docile executants of the Caudillo's wishes' is open to question: thus, many Falangists were notorious black marketeers, corrupt in local government and, as in the case of vertical syndicates organizer Salvador Merino, too radical.[16] These vertical syndicates demonstrate the fact that this bureaucratic state learned much from the economic policy of Fascist Italy. These lessons also included autarky, the Labour Charter establishing rights and duties of workers (1938), the 'Battle for Wheat' and the INI, a source of state investment for industry (1941). The Falangist Sección Femenina organized Franco's Social Service programme, and 're-educated' women in their traditional roles, analogous to the Nazi Kinder, Kirche, Küche. Rivera had argued that 'the family' was crucial to national strength. Indeed, as Grugel and Rees, for example, have highlighted, the Franco regime banned not only divorce but, along with all Catholic countries, contraception. As in Mussolini's Italy and the Third Reich, awards were given as incentive to produce large families, though, again as in Fascist Italy, the 'Battle of Births' was lost. Laws discouraging female 'employment' were passed and there was now an 'extreme form of patriarchal rule based on an ideology of separate spheres'.[17]

Through the voluntary Youth Front founded in 1940 (Pelayos aged 7–10, Fléchas 11–14, Cadetes 15–18) Falangists instilled political doctrine. The compulsory Falangist students' union, however, was to prove a radical source of anti-Franco opposition. In further contrast, Falangists such as the soon to be disaffected poet Dionisio Ridruejo occupied top positions in the Franco propaganda machine, press, radio, film, theatre, and so on, and its corollary, censorship. Falangists also enacted high-profile propaganda in another vital sense: well-orchestrated parades and rallies affirming mass support for the Caudillo with their fascist salute and conspicuous blue shirts.

The April 1937 Decree of Unification, which established the FET and diluted Rivera's Falange within a Francoist movement, lived up to

Rivera's fear of 'the establishment of a false, conservative fascism without revolutionary courage and young blood'. Both Griffin and Kedward have offered succinct definitions of fascism's fate under Franco. Thus, for Griffin, Franco 'neutralized fascism's revolutionary impetus by absorption', while Kedward has concluded that 'In reality the Spanish Civil War was as much the graveyard of idealistic fascism as idealistic communism.'[18]

The word 'Tradicionalista', as in FET, was an overt reference to the Carlists. But it also implied that 'revolution' was the doctrine of the past, tradition the concept of the present – and of the future. Much to the chagrin of the Falange 'left', the compliant 'Franco-Falange' agreed. José Luis Arrese, Franco-Falangist Secretary-General of the FET in 1941–5, wrote, 'Spain – and may some who wear the blue shirt but hide the red shirt hear it quite well – will be nothing if it is not Catholic . . . we believe in God, Spain and Franco.'[19]

Arrese's reference to the Catholic Church underlines the fact that the Franco regime sought a broader national ideal than fascism alone could provide. Indeed, Carr and Fusi in *Spain: Dictatorship to Democracy* (1981) have pointed to the existence of seven 'families' attached with varying degrees of influence to Franco's regime. The original 'institutionalized families' were the army, Church and Falange, the first two often at odds with the third. There were also the 'political families'. These were 'integral Francoists' who defined themselves by Franco's person exclusively; monarchists, whose loyalty was not unconditional; technocrats ('experts'); and professionals (modernizers in the civil service and academia).

This diversity points to the changing nature of the regime over time. Thus, for example, Catholic organizations – the reactionary Association of National Catholic Propagandists and then the more forward-looking Opus Dei – came to replace the Falange from the mid-1940s as providers of the defining 'tone' of the regime and the precise needs of the system and its leader. This new tone reflected, in turn, changing international circumstances.

Although economic ties with the Allies were maintained, until 1942–3 Franco's foreign policy was predominantly pro-Axis. In fact, the Caudillo ideologically identified himself with that cause well beyond any 'watershed' and he continued to assist the Axis whenever possible.

Previously Minister of the Interior, the Falangist Ramón Serrano Suñer became Foreign Minister in 1940. Franco's brother-in-law, Serrano was more an admirer of Mussolini than the Nazis. However, successful *Blitzkriegs* against Poland and the Western continental democracies showed imperial Nazism in the ascendant. So did initial German triumphs against the Soviet Union, to which the Falangist Blue Division lent ardent, and sacrificial, support. Serrano's fall from power in 1942 was due more to domestic tensions than to the turn of the wartime tide, but his dismissal is nevertheless symbolic of the Falange's own fall from grace.

Axis setbacks from 1942 encouraged Franco to camouflage his intuitive empathy for Hitler and Mussolini. However, despite the installation of a 'Cortes' in 1943, the 'Catholicization' of the regime and Franco's cordial greetings to Churchill and recognition of De Gaulle's provisional government following the war, Franco's own regime was still perceived as 'fascist'. Therefore, the United Nations Organization closed its doors to the Caudillo. But there was to be no coup against him. He had not ruled out an eventual restoration of the Spanish monarchy. Moreover, and more significantly in the shorter term, his 'fascist' regime would prove useful as a Cold War ally against communism. In this sense, 'fascism' and democracy shared a common identity.

Roger Griffin has described the Franco system as 'a stagnant neo-conservative regime . . . with no genuine commitment to create a national community'.[20] Indeed, there is a problem in equating years of unemployment, hunger, poverty, fear and vindictiveness with regenerating the nation's health. But revulsion against Franco's self-righteous cruelty is offset by uneasy admiration for his consummate statecraft: it would not have remained 'Franco's regime' without the Caudillo's unerring skill at balancing factions and interests and his adjustments to change. It is apparent that Franco's regime did indeed demonstrate fascist tendencies, both ideologically and institutionally, though always, as was the intention, on Franco's terms.

Questions

1. What grounds did the Falange have for disillusionment with the Franco dictatorship?
2. Why has the term 'elite pluralism' (Linz) been used to describe Franco's regime?

SOURCES

1. ASPECTS OF FRANCOISM

Source A (i): from Franco's Unification Decree, 19 April 1937.

In Spain as in other countries where there are totalitarian regimes, traditional forces are now beginning to integrate themselves with the new forces. The Falange Española has attracted masses of young people . . . and has provided a new political and heroic framework for the present and a promise of Spanish fulfilment in the future. The Requetés, in addition to possessing martial qualities, have served through the centuries as the sacred repository of Spanish tradition and of Catholic spirituality, which have been the principal formative elements of our nationality . . .

The Movement that we lead today is . . . in the process of elaboration, subject to constant revision and improvement, as reality may counsel. It is not rigid or static, but flexible. Therefore, as a movement it has undergone different stages [of development].

Abandoning that preoccupation with doctrine, we bring an effective democracy, bearing to the people what really interests them: seeing and feeling themselves governed [by men with] an aspiration for integral justice, as much in the moral order as in the socio-economic realm.

Source A (ii): Franco's power within the FET.

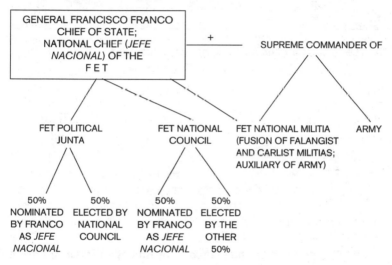

Source B: political background or identification of members of Franco's cabinets, January 1938–July 1962.

	Total	% of
Falange		
Falange with no previous political background	8	12
Falange with CEDA background, e.g. S. Suñer	5	7
Technical (experts) with Falangist orientation	4	6
Total Falange	17	25

Carlist	3	4.5
Acción Española (once led by Calvo Sotelo) and non-Carlist monarchist	2	3
Civil figures of the Miguel Primo de Rivera dictatorship	3	4.5
Political Catholicism, e.g. ACNP; Christian Democrat	3	4.5
Opus Dei	3	4.5
Technical or civil service apolitical	10	15
Military		
With Falangist leanings, e.g. Gen. Yagüe	3	4.5
With Carlist leanings	1	1.5
With Acción Española or Opus Dei ties	2	3
With CEDA background	2	3
Former office-holders under Miguel Primo de Rivera	2	3
With no particular identification	16	24
Total military	26	39
Total	67	100

Source C: the Caudillo's balancing act, according to the German Ambassador to the Franco regime, May 1938.

[Franco] has very cleverly succeeded, with the advice of his brother-in-law . . . in not making enemies of any of the parties represented in the Unity Party that were previously independent and hostile to one another . . . but, on the other hand, also in not favouring any one of them that might thus grow too strong . . . It is therefore comprehensible that, depending on the party allegiance of the person concerned, one is just as apt to hear the opinion in Spain that 'Franco is entirely a creature of the Falange,' as that 'Franco has sold himself completely to the reaction,' or 'Franco is a proven monarchist,' or 'He is completely under the influence of the Church.'

Source D: extracts from the Franco government's Labour Charter, 1938.

Reviving the Catholic tradition of social justice . . . The State . . . an instrument wholly at the service of the entire Nation . . . embarks upon the task of carrying out, with a disciplined constructive and soberly religious demeanour, the revolution that Spain is achieving to ensure that Spaniards may once more possess, for good and all, their Country, Bread and Justice . . .

Basing itself on the postulate that Spain is one and indivisible as regards her destiny, it hereby declares its aim to make Spanish industry . . . one and indivisible, so that it may minister to the needs of the country and uphold the instruments of its power . . .

The State values and exalts **work** ... and ... will protect it with all the force of the law, showing it the greatest consideration and making it compatible with other individual, family and social ends ...

The artisan, who is a living heritage of a glorious guild past, will be fostered and efficiently protected, as being a complete embodiment of the human person in his work and representing a form of production equally distant from capitalist concentration and gregarious Marxism ...

The State will guarantee to **tenants** continuity in cultivating their land by means of long-term contracts to safeguard them against unjustified eviction ... The State aspires to find ways and means to cause the land to pass, on fair terms, into the hands of those who work it directly ...

There will be an increase in **social insurances** against old age, disablement, maternity, work accidents, professional sicknesses, consumption and unemployment, the ultimate aim being the establishment of total insurance ...

Individual or collective acts that in any way **disturb normal production** or attempt to do so will be considered as ... treason against the Country ...

The State recognizes and protects **private property** as a natural means for fulfilling individual, family and social functions. All forms of property are subordinate to the supreme interests of the nation ...

All factors of economy will be incorporated, by branches of production or services, in vertical Guilds. The liberal and technical professions will be similarly organized ...

The officials of the Guilds will necessarily be chosen from the active members of the Spanish Traditionalist Phalanx (FET).

Source E: Dionisio Ridruejo (in 1938 Franco's propaganda chief) interviewed by Ronald Fraser in the 1970s.

The charter had very concrete origins: the Italians demanded it, maintaining that it was necessary to give the new state a more progressive social outlook and to remove suspicion that it was simply a reactionary regime. It was one of the very few times that the Italians intervened in the internal politics of the new regime, unlike the Germans.

The latter's main concern was repayment of their aid. I heard Serrano Suñer relate privately how German pressure became so great at one time that Franco said he would renounce German aid entirely and, if need be, fight the war as a guerrilla operation. 'We shall win the war in whatever way we can, for I am not prepared to sell any part of the national territory.'

Questions

1. How far does the language and tone of Source A (i) suggest that Franco's priority was a broad basis of support for the Unification Decree? (4)
2. In what senses does Source D suggest that the Labour Charter could be seen as the Unification Decree's economic and social equivalent? (4)
*3. Assess the value of Source B as evidence for the composition of Franco's cabinets. (8)
4. 'The new Spanish State will be a true democracy in which all citizens will participate in the government by means of their professional activity and their specific function' (Franco, July 1937). On the basis of your own research, how adequate a portrayal do you think these sources provide of Nationalist Spain during the Civil War? (9)

Worked answer

*3. [Lock in to the key word 'assess' – critical evaluation is needed. The challenge is to balance the table's strengths with its weaknesses.]

The time-scale of Source B is twenty-four years, during which time Franco presided over six cabinets. Source B begs the question: how consistent was the representation of each listed group, and in what posts? Even so, the source does point up the eclecticism of Franco's cabinets, the regime's 'elite pluralism' (Juan J. Linz). It also shows which groups were and were not strongly represented numerically. Those that were are likely to have had more than one seat on more than one cabinet. In fact, cabinets ranged from thirteen to nineteen members during this period, with an average size of fifteen. Source B also shows the military having the highest percentage as a group but that in terms of background it was diverse. We can also see that the highest percentage within the army (24 per cent) has no particular identity beyond loyalty to Franco. On the other hand, Source B demonstrates that the Falange, with a military and non-military combined total of 29.5 per cent, had the highest proportion in cabinet of those with a political profile beyond their 'Francoism'. There were actually three Falangists in the first cabinet to August 1939; doubling to six in the second to May 1941; and reducing to four in the third to July 1945. There remained a nominally Falangist component through to 1962 and beyond.

Source B also shows evidence of continuity with the pre-Franco era, including monarchists, ex-CEDA and ex-ministers of the Miguel Primo de Rivera dictatorship (1923–30). One of the latter, the aged but ruthless General Martínez Anido, died in 1938 while in office – the sort of 'change within a cabinet' concealed by Source B. Nor does Source B tell us anything of the formative Nationalist juntas (1936–7) or governments post-July 1962, a period of increasing dissent. Some of the terminology requires explanation, for example, Acción Española (an extreme monarchist group) and Opus Dei (Roman Catholic modernizers). And we are not told when Opus Dei acquired a significant voice for change. However, Source B does suggest strongly that Franco's cabinets combined breadth with concentration and that they were a coalition of talents and traditions serving Franco's will. Some caution is necessary concerning the military: it never made up more than 50 per cent of any cabinet and a military monopoly was precluded by the broad spectrum of interests that Franco sought to keep on board. On the other hand, the military's influence reached beyond cabinet, as did that of the Falange.

SOURCES

2. THE OUTCOME OF THE SPANISH CIVIL WAR

Source F: from the Diary of Count Ciano, Italian Foreign Minister.

March 28 1939: Madrid has fallen and with the capital all the other cities of Red Spain. The war is over. It is a new, formidable victory for Fascism, perhaps the greatest one so far . . .

Demonstrations in the Piazza Venezia because of the fall of Madrid. The Duce is overjoyed . . .

June 5 1939: Departure for Naples. Serrano Suñer arrives with the Duke of Aosta . . . Serrano Suñer clasps my hands for a long time and repeats words of gratitude for what Italy has done and her way of doing it. I embrace Gambara; through him I clasp to my breast every one of those who return and every one of those who remain in Spain, the guardians of a friendship and performers of a task which will produce glorious results.

I have a long conference with Serrano Suñer while we are driving through the streets of Naples. We touch on many points: . . . Spain fears a war in the near future because she is to-day at the end of her resources. In certain regions there is famine. If she can have two or preferably three years, she can reconstitute herself and complete her military preparations. Spain will be at the side of the Axis because she will be guided by feeling and by reason. A neutral Spain would, in any event, be destined to a future of poverty and humiliation . . . Serrano Suñer was very glad to learn that we and the Germans also wish to postpone the conflict for some years.

Source G: 'The Spaniard' gives evidence: from *The Trial of Mussolini* by 'Cassius' (Michael Foot), 1943.

Spain was defeated in London and Paris, where ignorant men believed that the peace of Europe could be sustained even if Mussolini conquered and where cowardly men believed that the freedom of Europe could be salvaged even if Spain became a corpse. It was by no act of the statesmen in London that Mussolini was prevented from gaining the swiftest and what would have been the most menacing of his triumphs. That service was performed by ragged ill-equipped armies, sometimes called 'scum'; and not merely were those armies deprived of the right to buy weapons; they had to fight against a Mussolini whose 'perfect good faith' was applauded in the British House of Commons even while his soldiers were battling to retrieve the bloody check administered to them before the gates of Madrid in 1936. To the blind eyes and stony hearts of some gentlemen in London, Mussolini was a better friend of peace than Dr Negrin, who obstinately refused to perform for his country the task discharged for France by Pétain in 1940. And while Count Grandi was being received in the salons of Mayfair, other Italians of the International Brigade were helping to win a battle at Guadalajara.

Source H: Dionisio Ridruejo, Falangist 'old shirt' and Franco's propaganda chief, interviewed by Ronald Fraser in the 1970s.

I was coming to realize that the revolution we had hoped to make was impossible. Eighty per cent of those being executed in the rearguard were workers. The repression was aimed at decimating the working class, destroying its power. In eliminating those whom our revolution was to benefit, the purpose of the revolution itself was itself eliminated. The reasoning behind the necessity for the purge was the sophism (shared moreover by both sides) that the enemy was a *minority* which was forcing the great mass of those on the other side to fight. Destroy that minority and order would be restored . . . It was a class war. Not everyone, certainly not the petty bourgeoisie on the nationalist side, recognized it as such, or they would have been on the other side. But the ruling class certainly knew it. Franco was its most lucid exponent.

Source I: from *The Face of Spain* by Gerald Brenan, 1950.

In a Madrid hotel the valet de chambre had been caught by the Civil War in Madrid where his sympathies had lain with the Nationalists, yet the picture he painted of present conditions was sombre in the extreme. The black market, he declared, was the only business in the country that was flourishing. Everyone from the highest authority down was in it. As he waited at the police post he would see lorries belonging to the Army or the Falange packed with black market goods pass without stopping . . .

[Wages] and salaries are a fraction of what they are with us. There has been a severe inflation and everyone except the landowners and nouveaux riches are finding it hard to make ends meet...

One of the things that most astonishes me in Madrid is the amount of building that has been done since the Civil War. Everywhere one sees new blocks of flats, business premises, ministries... one has to search hard to find any trace of the ruins of war...

[Near Torremolinos] we had not been in the house five minutes before Mr Washbrook began to explode with indignation... The condition of the working class was intolerable. Their wages were barely sufficient to keep them alive and the minute they lost their work they starved. The folly of the Government at allowing such a state of affairs was unbelievable... This was not a dictatorship but a free for all regime in which no-one thought of anything but feathering his own nest... 'The other day', said Mrs Washbrook, 'a man on the bus put the matter well. "General Franco", he said, "is a really great man. He is teaching Spaniards a wonderful thing – how to live without eating."'

How do the working class who cannot afford to live on the black market manage to keep alive? One way is by having extra ration books. New births are registered that have not occurred, deaths are concealed and so forth. There is even a trade in ration books.

Questions

1. Identify (a) Serrano Suñer (Source F); (b) Pétain (Source G). (2)
2. What issues are raised by the origins and contents of Source G as an explanation for the Republic's defeat? (4)
3. What contrasting perspectives are offered by Sources H and I on the impact of Franco's rule? (4)
*4. How accurate do you consider Source F in its comments on the outcome of the Spanish Civil War? (7)
5. Using these sources and your own knowledge, discuss the view that the outcome of Franco's victory in the Spanish Civil War was 'a perpetuation of terror rather than national renewal'. (8)

Worked answer

*4. [Because this is evaluative, avoid boxing yourself in at the beginning and limiting yourself to arguing only *for* 'accuracy' or *against* it. Also comment on the nature of the source.]

Ciano is able to comment reliably on the immediate outcome of the war. Beyond that, we must depend to some extent on hindsight – out of

Ciano's reach when he wrote these entries on 28 March and 5 June 1939. On the other hand, Ciano's final comment on the postponement of war, coming only two weeks after the Pact of Steel in which Germany had failed to give Italy such guarantees, can be read either as self-delusion or as desperation not to weaken the close ties he perceived to exist between Italy and Spain. Elsewhere, the extracts suggest that Ciano is on a 'high', projecting a celebration of military and diplomatic triumph for the benefit of his own self-esteem, his Duce and future generations of admirers.

In the 28 March entry Ciano's reference to a 'new, formidable victory for Fascism' is right to the extent that Italian Fascist help had played a vital part in Franco's defeat of the Spanish Republic. As a result of that victory the European balance of power had moved further towards nationalist dictatorships. But was Franco's regime 'fascist' and was that victory truly 'formidable' and 'perhaps the greatest so far'? The latter claim is understandable in that Fascism's victory in the earlier Abyssinian War had delivered rather shallow proof of Italy's prowess. In Spain, on the other hand, the demands of combat had been much tougher and the adjective 'formidable' more appropriately describes the cost of intervention to the Italian economy, which Denis Mack Smith has estimated as twice Italy's annual military budget.[21] This in turn throws into doubt those 'glorious results' referred to on 5 June. Spain joined the Anti-Comintern Pact in March 1939; but how deeply, despite Ciano's effusive picture of relations between Serrano Suñer and himself, did friendship penetrate between Spain and Italy? To what extent was Franco's Spain 'at the side of the Axis . . . by feeling and by reason'? Franco bonded psychologically with the Axis cause and gave as much material assistance as he could afford. But his international relations were multilateral. Economic ties with Britain remained. The limitations of his active commitment to the Axis are further shown by the succession of 'flags' flown by Spain between September 1939 and October 1943: neutrality; non-belligerence; moral belligerence; neutrality.

The extent of friendship connects also with the 'gratitude' Ciano says was affirmed by Spain's Foreign Minister 'for what Italy has done and her way of doing it'. The inventory of Italian aid is mind-boggling, and, subsequent to the airlift of Franco's troops to the mainland in July and August 1936, Italy had a high-profile role in the rebels' victorious campaigns. But this profile may have been too high. Franco resented boastful and condescending Italian generals and he recoiled both at the Italian terror bombing of Barcelona and the humane surrender terms the Italians granted the Basques, which Franco promptly revoked.

Seen in context, it might be expected that an element of melodrama and distortion would intrude into these extracts. With hindsight, some misgivings about them are equally predictable. In compensation, however, Source F offers not only Ciano's vivid impression of the 'historical moment' as it occurs, but some true-to-life insights into the post-war aims and aspirations of Fascist Italy and Francoist Spain.

NOTES AND SOURCES

1. THE PRIMO DE RIVERA DICTATORSHIP AND THE FALL OF THE MONARCHY

1. H. Thomas: *The Spanish Civil War* (Harmondsworth, 1977), p. 26
2. S. Payne: *Basque Nationalism* (Reno, 1975), p. 103
3. R. Carr: *Spain 1808–1975* (Oxford, 1982), p. 102
4. A. Balcells: *Catalan Nationalism Past and Present* (trans. J. Hall, Basingstoke, 1996), p. 88
5. G. Brenan: *The Spanish Labyrinth* (Cambridge, 1950/90), p. 78
6. H. Thomas: op. cit., pp. 29, 26
7. S. Ben-Ami: The Republican 'take-over': prelude to catastrophe?, in P. Preston, ed., *Revolution and War in Spain 1931–1939* (London, 1984), p. 15
8. G. Jackson: The Azaña regime in perspective (Spain, 1931–1933), in S. Payne, ed., *Politics and Society in Twentieth Century Spain* (New York, 1976), p. 81; P. Preston: *The Coming of the Spanish Civil War* (London, 2nd edn, 1994), p. 79
9. R. Carr: op. cit., p. 475
10. J.P. Fusi: The Basque Question, in P. Preston, ed., *Revolution and War*, p. 197
11. G. Brenan: op. cit., p. 85
12. M. Blinkhorn: War on two fronts: politics and society in Navarre 1931–36, in P. Preston, ed., *Revolution and War*, p. 79
13. H. Thomas: op. cit., p. 98
14. G. Esenwein and A. Shubert: *Spain at War* (Harlow, 1995), p. 76
15. R. Carr: op. cit., p. 645
16. G. Brenan: op. cit., p. 85
Source A: Manuel Azaña: Caciquismo and Democracy (trans. T. Rees, Exeter University), in *España*, 13 October 1923.
Source B: H. Gannes and T. Repard: *Spain in Revolt* (London, 1936), pp. 39–40.

Source C: Franz Borkenau: *The Spanish Cockpit* (London, 1937), pp. 40–1.

Source D: W. Foss and C. Gerahty: *The Spanish Arena* (London, 1938), pp. 53–5.

Source E: Duchess of Atholl: *Searchlight on Spain* (Harmondsworth, 1938), pp. 19–20.

Source F: H. Gannes and T. Repard: op. cit., pp. 42–3.

Source G: W. Foss and C. Gerahty: op. cit., pp. 58–9.

Source H: F. Borkenau: op. cit., p. 46.

Source I: M. Azaña: Speech to the Republican Action Party (trans. J.W.D. Trythall, York University), 17 July 1931.

2. THE SECOND REPUBLIC

1. P. Preston: The Agrarian War in the South, in P. Preston, ed., *Revolution and War*, pp. 175–6

2. H. Graham: Women and Social Change, in H. Graham and J. Labanyi, eds, *Spanish Cultural Studies: An Introduction* (Oxford, 1995), p. 109

3. A. Balcells: op. cit., pp. 108–9; N. Jones: Regionalism and Revolution in Catalonia, in P. Preston, ed., *Revolution and War*, p. 108

4. P. Preston: *Coming of the Spanish Civil War*, p. 180

5. F. Lannon: The Church's crusade against the Republic, in P. Preston, ed., *Revolution and War*, e.g. p. 52

6. P. Preston: *Coming of the Spanish Civil War*, p. 206

7. X.T. Gómez: The Popular Front elections in Spain, 1936, in S. Payne, ed., *Politics and Society*, pp. 93–119. On Calvo Sotelo's views see R. Carr: op. cit., p. 644

8. P. Preston: *Coming of the Spanish Civil War*, p. 239

9. Quoted in H. Gannes and T. Repard: *Spain in Revolt* (London, 1936), p. 121

10. G. Brenan: op. cit., especially pp. 301–2

11. P. Preston: *Coming of the Spanish Civil War*, p. 272

12. S. Payne, ed.: *Politics and Society*, pp. 120–44

Source A: H. Gannes and T. Repard: op. cit., pp. 125–6.

Source B: Translated by Alun Kenwood, in A. Kenwood, ed., *The Spanish Civil War: A Cultural and Historical Reader* (Oxford, 1993), pp. 49–52.

Source C: In S. Payne: *The Spanish Revolution* (London, 1970), pp. 178–9.

Source D: ibid.: pp. 188–9.

Source E: Duchess of Atholl: op. cit., p.75.

Source F: *El Debate* (trans. T. Rees, Exeter University), 1 January 1932.

Source G: ibid.: 23 October 1932.
Source H: A. Koestler: *Spanish Testament* (London, 1937), pp. 63–5
Source I: Translated by A. Kenwood, in A. Kenwood, ed., op. cit., pp. 48–9.
Source J: R. Fraser: *Blood of Spain* (London, 1979/94), p. 91.

3. THE MILITARY RISING

1. G. Hills: *The Battle for Madrid* (London, 1976), p. 26
2. P. Preston: *Franco* (London, 1993), pp. 104–6
3. H. Thomas: op. cit., p. 202
4. See, for example, S. Ellwood: *Franco* (London, 1993), pp. 52–8
5. H. Thomas: op. cit., p. 94
6. M. Alpert: Soldiers, politics and war, in P. Preston, ed., *Revolution and War*, pp. 203–4
7. R. Carr: op. cit., p. 650
8. P. Preston: *A Concise History of the Spanish Civil War* (London, 1996), p. 31
9. P. Preston: *Franco*, p. 146; H. Thomas: op. cit., p. 95; G. Hills, op. cit., pp. 32–3
10. P. Preston: *Coming of the Spanish Civil War*, p. 201
11. G. Hills: op. cit., p. 42
12. S. Payne: *Spanish Revolution*, p. 205
13. R. Fraser: *Blood of Spain* (London, 1994 edn), p. 568; Preston, *Coming of the Spanish Civil War*, p. 189
14. G. Esenwein and A. Shubert: op. cit., pp. 73, 69
15. Students may wish to research Koestler's political background further as he is a key source for this period.

Source A: B. Crozier: *Franco, A Biographical History* (London, 1967), p. 513.
Source B: From an English edition of the 'Joint Letter of the Spanish Bishops to the Bishops of the Whole World Concerning the War in Spain', published by the Catholic Truth Society (London, 1937).
Source C: Harold G. Cardozo: *March of a Nation – My Year of Spain's Civil War* (London, 1937), pp. 150–1, 153.
Source D: Julio Alvarez del Vayo: *Freedom's Battle* (London, 1940), pp. 24–5, 28.
Source E: Translated by A. Kenwood, in A. Kenwood, ed., op. cit., pp. 90–1.
Source F: Goronwy Rees: Europe and Spain (7.8.36), in Charles Moore and Christopher Hawtree, eds, *1936, As Recorded by the Spectator* (London, 1986).
Source G: In D. Smyth: *Reflex Reaction – Germany and the Onset of*

the Spanish Civil War, in P. Preston, ed., Revolution and War, p. 253.

Source H: P. Knight: The Spanish Civil War (Basingstoke, 1991), p.65.

Source I: Quoted in P. Preston: Mussolini's Spanish adventure: from limited risk to war, in P. Preston and A. McKenzie (eds), The Republic Besieged (Edinburgh, 1996), pp. 48–9.

Source J: A. Koestler: op. cit., pp. 96–7, 146.

4. THE REPUBLIC'S RESPONSE

1. G. Hills: op. cit., p. 49
2. R. Kisch: They Shall Not Pass (London, 1974), p. 43
3. S. Payne: Spanish Revolution, p. 316; G. Hills: op. cit., p. 55
4. R. Fraser: op. cit., p. 118
5. See, for example, C. Leitz: Nazi Germany's intervention in the Spanish Civil War, in P. Preston and A. McKenzie, eds, op. cit., pp. 53–85
6. Duchess of Atholl: op. cit., p. 86
7. S. Payne: Spanish Revolution, p. 314
8. G. Hills: op. cit., p. 86
9. ibid.: p. 134
10. G. Jackson: A Concise History of the Spanish Civil War (London, 1980 edn), p. 90
11. M. Alpert: Soldiers, politics and war, pp. 219–20
12. P. Preston: Franco, p. 211
13. S. Payne: Spanish Revolution, pp. 321–2; M. Alpert: Soldiers, politics and war, pp. 207, 211
14. G. Hills: op. cit., p. 60
15. M. Alpert: Soldiers, politics and war, pp. 213–14
16. S. Payne: Spanish Revolution, p. 340
17. H. Graham: Spain and Europe: the view from the periphery, in The Historical Journal, 35, 4 (1992), p. 973. See books by G. Howson, for example, Arms for Spain: The Untold Story of the Spanish Civil War (London, 1998)
18. P. Preston: Concise History, p. 137

Source A: R. Rocker: The Tragedy of Spain (New York, 1937), p. 14. Internet: http://www.xchange.anarki.net /~huelga/life.htm.

Source B: ibid.: p. 1.

Source C: G. Orwell: Homage to Catalonia (London, 1938; this edn 1989) pp. 190–1.

Source D: G. Leval: Collectives in Spain (London, 1938). Internet: http://calvin.pitzer.edu /~dward/Anarchist-Archives/leval/. collectives.html.

Source E: A. Kenwood, ed., op. cit., p. 270.

5. INTERVENTION AND NON-INTERVENTION: IDEALISM OR EXPEDIENCY?

1. G. Jackson: *Concise History*, p. 168
2. D. Smyth: Germany and the onset of the Spanish Civil War, in P. Preston, ed., *Revolution and War*, p. 243
3. C. Leitz: in P. Preston and A. McKenzie, eds, op. cit., p. 63
4. M. Alpert: *A New International History of the Spanish Civil War* (Basingstoke, 1994), p. 80
5. P.M.H. Bell: *The Origins of the Second World War in Europe* (London, 2nd edn 1997), p. 240
6. P. Preston: *Franco*, p. 238
7. ibid.: p. 289
8. H. Thomas: op. cit., p. 941; D. Smyth in P. Preston: *Revolution and War*, p. 257; P. Preston: *Franco*, p. 314
9. H. Thomas: op. cit., p. 975
10. C. Leitz in P. Preston and A. McKenzie, eds, op. cit., p. 72
11. D. Smyth in P. Preston, *Revolution and War*, p. 264, fn. 53
12. ibid.: p. 257; M. Alpert: *New International History*, p. 96
13. E. Moradiellos: The gentle general: the official British perception of General Franco during the Spanish Civil War, in P. Preston and A. McKenzie, eds, op. cit., pp. 1–19
14. A. Adamthwaite: *Grandeur and Misery: France's Bid for Power in Europe 1914–1940* (London, 1995), p. 142
15. Quoted in M. Alpert: *New International History*, p. 48
16. ibid.: p. 119
17. ibid.: p. 44
18. E. Weber: *The Hollow Years: France in the 1930s* (London, 1996), p. 168
19. T. Buchanan: *Britain and the Spanish Civil War* (Cambridge, 1997)
20. ibid.: p. 120
21. Referring to G.L. Steer: *The Tree of Gernika: A Field Study of Modern War* (London, 1938)
22. As a postscript to this section, research the history and message of Picasso's painting *Guernica*, if possible comparing it with other artistic statements about the Spanish Civil War such as Robert Motherwell's series of abstract paintings *Elegies to the Spanish Republic.*

Source A: *Changing Times* CD-rom (News Multimedia, 1993).
Source B: W. Foss and C. Gerahty: op. cit., p. 438.
Source C: Duchess of Atholl: op. cit., pp. 189–91.
Source D: H. Browne: *Spain's Civil War* (Harlow, 1996), pp. 125–6.
Source E: R. Fraser: op. cit., p. 401, fn.1.

Source F: L. Lee: *A Moment of War* (Harmondsworth, 1991), pp. 92–4.

Source G: Translated by Norman Denny, in A. Kenwood, ed., op. cit., pp. 258, 259–60.

Source H: E. Hemingway: *For Whom the Bell Tolls* (English edn; London, 1941), pp. 390–1.

Source I: W. Foss and C. Gerahty: op. cit., p. 393.

6. POLITICS ON THE REPUBLICAN SIDE AND THE ROLE OF THE SOVIET UNION

1. H. Thomas: op. cit., pp. 160–1
2. R. Carr: op. cit., p. 667; G. Esenwein and A. Shubert, op. cit., p. 220
3. M. Alpert: *New International History*, p. 74; D. Smyth: 'We Are With You . . .', in P. Preston and A. McKenzie, eds, op. cit., p. 89
4. J. Gurney: *Crusade in Spain* (London, 1974), p. 54
5. F. Borkenau: *The Spanish Cockpit* (London, 1937), p. 273. On Borkenau, see T. Buchanan: op. cit., pp. 166–7
6. G. Jackson, *Concise History*, p. 95; S. Payne: *Spanish Revolution*, p. 329; G. Hills: op. cit., p. 109
7. H. Thomas: op. cit., p. 480; D. Mitchell: *The Spanish Civil War* (London, 1982), p. 82; P. Preston, *Concise History*, pp. 122–3
8. F. Borkenau: op. cit., p. 268
9. G. Hills: op. cit., p. 166
10. N. Ascherson: *The Spanish Civil War* (script for Granada TV series, 1983, Part 5)
11. Quoted in R. Kisch: op. cit., p. 135
12. Quoted in D. Mitchell: op. cit., p. 73
13. E. Líster, speaking on *The Spanish Civil War* (Granada, 1983)
14. G.F. Kennan: *Soviet Foreign Policy 1917–1941* (Princeton, 1960), p. 27
15. R. Carr: op. cit., p. 663. On Republican propaganda, see the discussion in G. Esenwein and A. Shubert: op. cit., pp. 243–50
16. B. Bolloten: *The Spanish Civil War: Revolution and Counter-revolution* (North Carolina, 1991); A. Viñas: The financing of the Spanish Civil War, in P. Preston: *Revolution and War*; H. Graham: War, modernity and reform: the premiership of Juan Negrín, 1937–1939, in P. Preston and A. McKenzie, eds, op. cit., pp. 163–96
17. E. Malefakis: Internal political problems and loyalties: the Republican side in the Spanish Civil War, in S. Payne, ed., *Politics and Society*, especially pp. 148–51; R. Carr: op. cit., pp. 65, 67–8; G. Esenwein and A. Shubert, op. cit., pp. 209–10

18. S. Payne: *Basque Nationalism*, p. 195
19. A. Balcells: op. cit., p. 117; N. Ascherson: *Spanish Civil War*
20. H. Graham: War, Modernity and reform, pp. 185–6; R. Carr: op. cit., p. 662

Source A: R. Rocker: op. cit., p. 3.

Source B: P. Togliatti ('Ercoli') to the 'Secytariat of Cmr. Manuilski For Com. Dimitrov', 30 August 1937, cited in E.H. Carr: *The Comintern and the Spanish Civil War* (Basingstoke, 1984), pp. 91–2.

Source C: J. Gurney: op. cit., pp. 175–6.

Source D: Duchess of Atholl: op. cit., pp. 172, 216–17, 232.

Source E: ibid.: op. cit., pp. 341–4.

Source F: Largo Caballero to Stalin, Molotov and Voroshilov, Valencia, 12 January 1937, cited in E.H. Carr: op.cit., pp. 87–8.

Source G: R. Fraser: op. cit., p. 333.

Source H: R. Rocker: op. cit., pp. 2, 12.

Source I: G. Brenan: op. cit., pp. 325–6.

Source J: F. Borkenau: op. cit., pp. 290–3.

7. FRANCO AND FASCISM

1. G. Hills: op. cit., pp. 50–1; P. Preston: *Concise History*, p. 79
2. S. Payne: *Spanish Revolution*, p. 349
3. ibid.: p. 347
4. R. Carr: op. cit., p. 689
5. From *Spanish Civil War* (Granada, 1983). For a summary of conditions besetting the Republican home front, see H. Graham: War, Modernity and reform, pp. 194–6
6. R. Carr: op. cit., p. 683; Pilar Primo de Rivera filmed in 1982 for *Spanish Civil War* (Granada, 1983). For a balanced assessment of collectivization, see G. Esenwein and A. Shubert: op. cit., pp. 133–43
7. José Antonio Primo de Rivera speaking in English, *c.* 1933, from *Spanish Civil War* (Granada, 1983)
8. N. Ascherson: *Spanish Civil War*
9. A. Kenwood: op. cit., p. 92
10. S. Ellwood: op. cit., p. 149
11. R. Griffin: *The Nature of Fascism* (London, 1991), p. 123
12. Falange's Twenty-seven Points, Point III, in A. Kenwood: op. cit., p. 42
13. Chief of State's Inauguration Speech, October 1936, cited in Duchess of Atholl: op. cit., p. 250
14. M. Richards: Civil War, violence and the construction of Francoism, in P. Preston and A. McKenzie, eds, op. cit., pp. 204–5

15. P. Preston: Introduction, in P. Preston and A. McKenzie, eds, op. cit., p. xiv
16. E. de Blaye: *Franco and the Politics of Spain* (Harmondsworth, 1976), p. 459. Quotation is de Blaye's description of Hedilla's successors in the Falange leadership
17. J. Grugel and T. Rees: *Franco's Spain* (London, 1997), p. 134
18. R. Griffin: op. cit., p. 124; R. Kedward: *Fascism in Western Europe 1900–45* (London, 1973), p. 131
19. S. Payne: *Falange* (Stanford, 1961), p. 232
20. R. Griffin: op. cit., p. 104
21. D. Mack Smith: *Mussolini's Roman Empire* (Harmondsworth, 1977), p. 105

Source A: (i) P. Knight: op. cit., p. 94, and S. Payne: *Falange*, p. 169; (ii) Author.
Source B: Adapted from Juan J. Linz: *An Authoritarian Regime: Spain*, in S. Payne, ed., *Politics and Society in Twentieth Century Spain* (New York, 1976), p. 189.
Source C: S. Payne: *Falange*, p. 180.
Source D: Spanish Press Services, Ltd, 1938.
Source E: R. Fraser, op. cit., p. 470.
Source F: *Ciano's Diary 1939–1943* (London, 1947), pp. 57, 99–100.
Source G: M. Foot ('Cassius'): *The Trial of Mussolini* (London, 1943), pp. 66–7.
Source H: R. Fraser, op. cit., p. 320.
Source I: G. Brenan: *The Face of Spain* (London, 1950), quoted more fully in P. Knight, op. cit., pp. 128–9.

SELECT BIBLIOGRAPHY

PRIMARY SOURCES

Although most of Harry Browne's *Spain's Civil War* (2nd edn, London, 1996) is an established secondary work, the text includes bracketed references to the many document extracts that follow it. In contrast, Patricia Knight's *The Spanish Civil War* (Basingstoke, 1991) is document-centred, with source-related questions at the end of each chapter. Ronald Fraser's *Blood of Spain* (London, 1979/86) is built on testimony from the 300-plus eyewitnesses he interviewed in the 1970s, interwoven with his own commentary. In *Homage to Catalonia* (originally published 1938; Harmondsworth, 1989 edn) George Orwell shares his perceptions of the war in that region and its ramifications, and writes compellingly of his experiences with the POUM militia. Appendix II is a model of vigorous source analysis where Orwell dissects Communist press reports. Penguin Audiobooks have an abridged version of *Homage*. Many secondhand bookshops have 'search' systems for out-of-print books: David Mitchell's *The Spanish Civil War* (Granada, 1982), rich in reminiscences, photographs and full-colour posters; Jason Gurney's hard-hitting memoir *Crusade in Spain* (London, 1974), and Franz Borkenau's perceptive *The Spanish Cockpit* (London, 1937) are well worth rooting out. Gerald Brenan credited Franz Borkenau with a role in inspiring his 1943 book *The Spanish Labyrinth* (Cambridge, 2nd edn, 1950; since 1993 with a foreword by Raymond Carr). It has brief but valuable comment on the war, but most of it is on long- and short-term background. This includes the Primo de Rivera dictatorship (1923–30). *The Penguin Book of Spanish Civil War Verse* (Valentine

Cunningham, ed., Harmondsworth, 1996) has a useful in-depth introduction and includes Louis MacNeice's haunting 'And I Remember Spain'. A different concept is *The Spanish Civil War: A Cultural and Historical Reader* (A. Kenwood, ed., Oxford, 1993) which features 'responses' to the war, including Hispanic, British and American, in reportage, novels and poems. It also has political documents. In *Brother against Brother* (Robert Stradling, ed., Stroud, 1998) Frank Thomas relates his experiences fighting for the Nationalists.

SECONDARY SOURCES

Of the general surveys, Martin Blinkhorn's *Democracy and Civil War in Spain* (London, 1988) is succinct and clearly ordered. Paul Preston's *Concise History of the Spanish Civil War* (London, 1996) is a vivid evocation of the background and the conduct of the war itself, with an indispensable bibliographical essay. Patricia Knight's *The Spanish Civil War* is a recent contribution to the Access to History series (London, 1998).

Of the more in-depth accounts, Hugh Thomas's *The Spanish Civil War* (Harmondsworth, 3rd edn, 1977) also has useful preface, footnotes, maps and appendices. More recent are Raymond Carr's *Spanish Tragedy: The Civil War in Perspective* (London, 1993) and George Esenwein and Adrian Shubert's *Spain at War* (London, 1995), which considers long-term tensions in Spain and the degree of unity on the Republican and Nationalist sides. On the Second Republic, see Paul Preston's *The Coming of the Spanish Civil War* (London, 2nd edn, 1994), with close analysis of grassroots conflicts and the splits bedevilling the PSOE; and Stanley G. Payne's *Spain's First Democracy, The Second Republic 1931–1936* (Wisconsin, 1993). Raymond Carr's *Spain 1808–1975* (Oxford, 1982) combines breadth with depth and places the Republic in a longer-term perspective. On Republican politics and the Civil War there is Helen Graham's *Socialism and War: The Spanish Socialist Party in Power and Crisis 1936–39* (Cambridge, 1991), which examines how the Republican conduct of the war was undermined by power struggles involving the PSOE and the PCE. *Falange: A History of Spanish Fascism* by Stanley G. Payne (Stanford, 1961) has many primary-source quotations. While Michael Alpert's *A New International History of the*

Spanish Civil War (Basingstoke, 1994) confronts the contra-dictions of the Non-Intervention Committee and the behaviour of its members, in *Arms to Spain: The Untold Story of the Spanish Civil War* (London, 1998) Gerald Howson considers arms sales to the Republic. Tom Buchanan's *Britain and the Spanish Civil War* (Cambridge, 1997) analyses such issues as the stance of political parties, volunteers in Spain and the press. James K. Hopkins's *Into the Heart of the Fire: The British in the Spanish Civil War* (Stanford, 1998) draws on newly opened Russian archives and explores the wide range of identities of British volunteers. Interesting on American intellectuals and the war is James R. Mellow's *Ernest Hemingway: A Life without Consequences* (London, 1993).

Collections of essays include Paul Preston, ed., *Revolution and War in Spain 1931–1939* (London, 1984) and Paul Preston and Anne L. McKenzie, eds., *The Republic Besieged: Civil War in Spain 1936–1939* (Edinburgh, 1996). Also useful is Martin Blinkhorn, ed., *Spain in Conflict 1931–39: Democracy and its Enemies* (Wisconsin, 1986). A clear thematic survey of the Francoist system is *Franco's Spain* by Jean Grugel and Tim Rees (London, 1997). Biographies which complement each other are *Franco* by Sheelagh Ellwood and Paul Preston (both London, 1993). Paul Preston's collection *Comrades! Portraits from the Spanish Civil War* (London, 1999) includes essays on the Primo de Rivera siblings, Pilar and José Antonio. Arachnophiles will find websites to explore, for example, on posters in the Southworth Spanish Civil War Collection.

FILMS

The following is a selection of films with a Spanish Civil War theme or dimension. Those available on video are asterisked. The British Film Institute National Film and Television Archive has published a filmography, compiled by Luke McKernan (1996), of its Spanish Civil War holdings.

SPANISH EARTH (1937, USA)
Directed by Joris Ivens. Pro-Republican documentary. Commentary by Ernest Hemingway, then a leading figure in the Contemporary Historians group.

BLOCKADE (1938, USA)
Directed by the pro-Spanish Republican William Dieterle. *Blockade*'s Oscar nominated scriptwriter John Howard Lawson later became a victim of the McCarthyite witch-hunts against the left.

DAYS OF HOPE (*L'Espoir*) (1939, France)
Directed by André Malraux, who had flown for the Republicans. Set during the Teruel Campaign, many of the cast were actual combatants and Spanish filming was halted when Franco's forces took Barcelona.

RACE (*Raza*) (1941, Spain)
Directed by Saénz de Heredia (a cousin of José Antonio Primo de Rivera), whose brother was killed in 1936. Screenplay by General Franco. A family (based on Franco's) is divided by the Civil War.

FOR WHOM THE BELL TOLLS (1943, USA)
From the novel by Ernest Hemingway. Directed by Sam Wood.

An American demolitions expert fights alongside Republican guerrillas. Set during the Segovia Campaign, May 1937. Banned in Spain during the Franco regime.

CONFIDENTIAL AGENT (1945, USA)
Directed by Herman Shumlin, who, like Hemingway, belonged to Contemporary Historians. The film tells of a Frenchman's struggles to purchase much-needed fuel for the Republicans.

THE HUNT (*La Caza*) (1965, Spain)
Directed by the highly regarded Carlos Saura, the film is set during a hunting trip to the battle-scarred landscape of Toledo, whose Alcázar was famously besieged in 1936.

*THE SPIRIT OF THE BEEHIVE (1973, Spain)
Directed by Víctor Erice. One of two sisters befriends an escaped Republican prisoner. A film of innocence and experience.

THE LONG HOLIDAYS OF 36 (1976, Spain)
Directed by Jaime Camino at the close of the Franco era, this film is set in Barcelona among a family divided by the Civil War. A decade on, Camino made *Dragón Rapide* which contained a portrayal of General Franco.

*AY CARMELA! (1990, Spain)
Directed by Carlos Saura, this film focuses on a group of travelling entertainers captured by the Nationalists and required to perform for Franco. A potent mix of humour, hope and tragedy.

VACAS (*Cows*) (1991, Spain)
Directed by Julio Medem and set in the Basque Country among generations of Carlists. A strange, symbolic film about loyalty, conflict and tradition.

*LAND AND FREEDOM (1995, GB/Spain/Germany)
Directed by Ken Loach. An English volunteer fights with the POUM militia. Controversial, but a moving story with sharply observed training and combat scenes and a vigorous debate about whether to collectivize the land of the local nobleman.

INDEX

Atholl, Katharine, Duchess of 13,
28, 82, 84, 103
autarky; self-sufficiency 4, 58,
117
Azaña, Manuel: on *caciquismo* 11;
leads Left Republican Party
17; as Minister of War 16, 17,
35, 38, 39; succeeds Alcalá
Zamora as Prime Minister
(Oct 1931) **19**; Prime Minister
1936 (Feb–May) 21, 25, 30,
33, **36**, 39, 41, 42, 45;
President (May 1936–March
1939) 26, 30, 60

Badajoz **20**, 49, **51**, 53, 73, 118
Baldwin, Stanley 78, 79
Balearic Is. 38, 48, 49, 50, **51**, 54
Barcelona: to 1931 (April) **1**, , 5,
15; during Second Republic
21; in Civil War **52**, 53–4, 75,
87, **91**, **92**, **93**, 100, 103, 114,
118, 128, 142
Basque Country: to1931 (April) 4;
during Second Republic **36**; in
Civil War **51**, 74, 75, 84, 86,
99–100, 116, 128, 142; *see
also* Bilbao; Guernica; Vizcaya
campaign
Beimler, Hans (International
Brigades) 88
Belchite, battle of (Aragón, 1937)
88, 103, 113
Berenguer, Gen. Damaso 8, 10, 37
Besteiro, Julián 28
Bilbao **52**, 53, 54, 74, 76, 77, 82,
86, 113
Bishops' Pastoral Letter on the
Constitution (1931) 30–1,
33–4
Blum, Léon **71**, 79
Borkenau, Franz 12, 13–16, 95,
96,108, 138
Brenan, Gerald 5, 8, 10, 25, 107,
126, 138
Britain: *see* United Kingdom
Brunete, battle of (1937) **52**, 58,
61, 74, **92**, 95, 96, 113
Buñuel, Luis 20
Burgos **51**, 55

caciques; *caciquismo* **2**, 3, 5, 11,
15
Cádiz **51**, **71**, **72**
Calvo Sotelo, José 4, 23, 24, 26,
32, 34, **36**, 38, 40, 43, 45,
122
Canary Is. **36**, 38, **51**
captains-general 3, 6
Carlists: to1931 (April) 7, 9, 142;
during Second Republic 9, 10,
23, **36**, 38, 40, 45, 54, 56,
122, 142; in Civil War 85,
111, 119, 122, 142; *see also
requetés*
Carrillo, Santiago 63
Cartagena 74, 94
casa del pueblo 64, 65
Casado, Col, Segismundo
(Republican) **94**, 98
Casares Quiroga, Santiago 26, 30,
36, 40, **52**, **91**
Castile **36**, 46, 47, **51**, 55
Castilblanco **20**
Castillo, José 40
Catalonia: to 1931 (April) **1**, 3, 4, 5,
13, 15; during Second
Republic **18**, **20**, 21, 22, 26,
29, **36**, 37; in Civil War **53**,
54, 63, 75, **93**, 96, 100, 102,
103, 107, 108, **111**, 113,
114, 116, 117
catastrophism 9, 33, 42, 43
Catholic Church: to1931 (April) 1,
2, 4, 9, 11, 12, 22; during
Second Republic 9, **19**, **20**,
22, 25, 30, 33, 37, 42, 44; in
Civil War 44, 62, 63, 82, 83,
84–5, 86, 87, 100, 113, 122;
after Civil War 119
CEDA **18**, **20**, 21–3, 24, 25, 31,
33, 40, 42, 43, **110**, **111**,
121–2,124
Chamberlain, Neville 78, 80, **93**
church burnings **20**, 25, 26
Churchill, Winston 120
Ciano, Count Galeazzo 48, 113,
125, 127–9
Civil Guard **2**, **20**, 38, 41, 42, 43,
45, 53–4, 57
CNT: to 1931 (April) 3; during